Scrappy Hooked Rugs

Making the Most of the Wool in Your Stash

By Bea Brock

Copyright © 2014 by Stackpole Books
Published by
STACKPOLE BOOKS
5067 Ritter Road
Mechanicsburg, PA 17055
www.stackpolebooks.com

www.rughookingmagazine.com

Printed in the United States of America

10 9 8 7 6 5 4 3

Cover design by Caroline M. Stover
Photographs by the author, unless otherwise noted

Library of Congress Cataloging-in-Publication Data

Brook, Bea.
  Scrappy hooked rugs : making the most of the wool in your stash / Bea
Brock.—First edition.
    pages cm
  ISBN 978-1-881982-95-1
  1. Rugs, Hooked. I. Title.
  TT850.B78 2014
  746,7'4—dc23
                                          2013041544

Contents

Acknowledgments

Staring at blank pages needing to be filled, it was in a mild state of anxiety and curiosity that I called Martha Reynolds in Dallas, Texas, to see if she might know some hookers in her area who might want to help me out on this project by hooking rugs. In taking on the project I was undeniably sure of one thing: I needed help. Martha sent an email to her guild explaining the situation and I met with a group of surprisingly generous women who listened intently about the work up ahead and was blessed by a response that was totally unexpected. Summoning courage, I asked a few other friends here and there around the state, and the spigot of generosity poured forth again and again. Rugs take a long time to make. We cherish them, hold on to most, and give some away as heartfelt mementos to precious friends and family. To hook a rug for someone else's project? Well, it is an amazing display of kindness and generosity and there is gratitude within me that will not die. Thank you in copious bunches to Alison Auckland, Judy Bruns, Jaci Clements, Ann Deane, Honey Gill, Janet Griffith, Karen Lea, Melody Lundquist, Brenda McGee, Teena Mills, Paty Parish Pitts, Gina Paschal, Martha Reynolds, Barbara Riley, Carol Rippa, Mary Ruelle, Ginger Smith, Janie Staples, and Linda Huntley Wills.

A special thanks to Tricia Travis and Bracken Village Ltd. for the great photography site. In the heat of a typical Texas morning, I could not have been more welcomed with cold bottled water and Tricia's assistance in setting up photos on the porch of Country Gatherings.

I have to confess of my lifelong character flaw of being ridiculously single-minded. I guess it gets things done in one area, but not so much in others. With that in mind, there are no limits to my appreciation and gratefulness for my sweet, kind, and loving husband who steamed a lot of vegetables for his evening dinner in the ensuing months. And to boot, he shared a lot of them with me. There is no lacking of support and encouragement in this wonderful family of mine that provides me with the room to be a little wacky sometimes and pursue my creative endeavors in between their comings and goings. To God be the glory!

Introduction

In my first steps of rug hooking—almost 20 years ago—I was attracted by the economy of using recycled goods. I foraged through resale shops amassing wool garments by the armful, equally delighted by wool's textural and color variety as by its compatibility with my budgetary concerns. Wool covered the best of both worlds! Looking back at this curious but humorous obsession, I realize now that the acquisition of all things textural is something that is peculiar to fiber crafters and artists everywhere. It's an expression of our love of the tactile.

Over the years this love has not dimmed. I can have a dyeing day, producing 30 to 40 yards of wool in a variety of colors, and I will still walk over to the dryer with anticipation of seeing and feeling the fruits of my labor. I gently sort the quarter-yard pieces into color groups, fold them precisely for display, stack them on the table, and admire them from a distance as well as fondle them at every passing. Nutty isn't it?

In my experiences with rug hookers around the United States, I have found a common thread. At hook-ins and other rug hooking events, heads turn to gaze at the myriad of yardage displayed among all the vendors. Color and tactile stimulation draw us like moths to the light. There are no bounds to this love of woolly things, and the appetites across the country have indeed been well satisfied. Who among us is not the keeper and manager of wool closets, wool cupboards, wool bins and baskets, wool shelves, even wool rooms where the manifestations of our lustful habits reside. Ever hear of the SABLE acronym? It stands for "stash acquisition beyond life expectancy." You are not alone!

What you may not know is that in the years of your stockpiling, you have amassed a collection that is uniquely yours. Like all of us, your personal color inclinations are evident in your ever-growing stash, and with the information in the pages ahead, you will be able to put some of that wool to use in your next and subsequent rugs.

Consider your wool collection a blessing. In these times when many of us are motivated to embrace more economic strategies for our finances, using what we already have on hand can be a deep source of satisfaction. Your wool stash no longer has to be a monument to your lack of purchasing restraint. In the pages ahead we will talk about how you can assess what you have and know how to use it. You will be overjoyed to see your collection with fresh eyes and produce rugs that speak to you in satisfying ways.

It is my most earnest intention to guide you through these pages with the hopes of empowering you to understand color and, perhaps, encourage you to cross the threshold into designing your own patterns. Give heed to the information contained herein, study the samples and rug photos, and you can begin to bridge the gap between a great wool stash and the best rugs to come. In my ongoing quest to encourage individual style, I implore you: give your heart and thoughts to those components herein that point you to what lives beneath the surface and is begging to live in full view in your work. The best of my wishes are poured out on the pages to accompany you to the next level in your rug hooking careers.—*Bea Brock*

What's In Your Wool Closet?

My wool is displayed in full view on four shelves and organized by color: (top to bottom, left to right) yellow greens to cooler greens; blues to purples; reds and rusts; and golds and neutrals.

I f you have been hooking rugs for a number of years, as I have, you very likely have collected quite a number of pieces of wool. Most of our closets contain multiple yard pieces, half-yard pieces, quarter-yard pieces, intact scraps left over from finished projects, and finally, the bane of a lot of rug hookers, the dreaded leftover strips or, as we affectionately call them, worms.

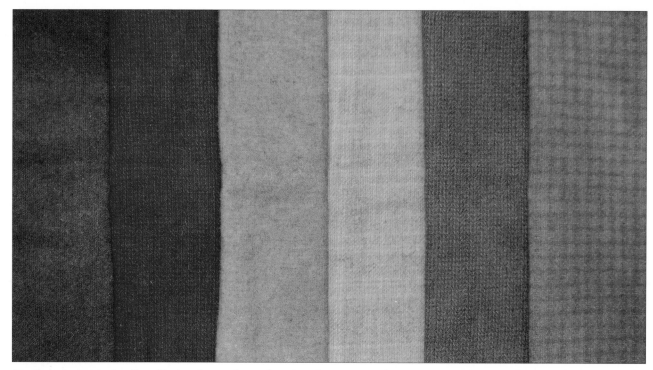

Use the primary (red, yellow, blue) and secondary colors (purple, orange, and green) as a starting point for organizing your wool into six color categories.

So here we are with this nonuniform assortment of supplies, scratching our heads about how best to store everything. Some of us are blessed with special rooms or closets to store it all, while many of us resort to under-the-bed boxes or armoires adapted with shelves for storage. And I am quite sure other (though still unknown to me) options exist. But the bigger issue I am attempting to bring up here is this: Is your storage system working for you?

If you really want to use what you have, then you have to know what you've got. Organization is your friend. Organization will save you time and frustration when you start looking for that perfect shade of gold that you just happened to remember purchasing three years ago at your local annual hook-in from "what's her name, the vendor." You can spend a lot of time scratching your head trying to think of which project you last used it in, toppling stacks, checking in old project bags, and really working up a sweat digging to the bottom of those baskets or boxes. I am not suggesting that we rug hookers go all out and establish a Dewey Decimal System for our wool, but having it accessible and visible at all times can really go a long way toward simplifying your thought processes when planning a new rug or making changes along the way.

I realize I am pushing the envelope here, but bear with me and see if just maybe a fractional upgrade on what I am going to suggest may be implemented for the sake of living at total peace and harmony with your hobby.

Ready?

Arrange your wool in color wheel order.

Okay, I said it. Are you rolling your eyes at me yet?

ORGANIZE BY COLOR

The most basic color wheel order uses the primary and secondary colors as your guide. In other words, start with red (primary), then purple, then blue (primary), then green, then yellow (primary) or gold, then orange or rust. Run the colors on your shelves from left to right all the way down the shelves. I do this at my vending events for two reasons: First, it looks great; second, if I am helping someone color plan a rug I know exactly where to go to find the color I am thinking would be perfect for his or her rug.

Now, putting your wool pieces in color order

If your stash is large, expand upon the six categories to include the variations within the color wheel.

within six categories is simple enough, but we all know that each group has so many distinctive variations. If your stash is significant, you will have to give thought to all those permutations that exist in shade and tone. For this reason, because of my extensive array of wool, I resort to categories that take into account a transitioning from one color to the next.

Here is a verbal sampling of how I begin on the left and work toward the right in shades and tones then downward.

1. Reds: Begin with bright orangey reds, then coral reds, crayon reds, blue garnet-like reds, wines, and maroons. They are all in the red family.

2. Purples: Start with the reddish plums, then move to purples, violets, and blue violets.

3. Blues: Put cobalt on the shelf first, then add royal blue, denim blue, indigo, peacock blues, and turquoises.

4. Greens: Place teal greens, spruce greens, leaf green, sage green, olive green, lime green, and chartreuse.

5. Yellows: Look for lemon yellow, crayon yellow, gold, and amber.

6. Oranges: This final color family will lead right back to reds: rusts, pumpkin, orange, and coral.

It doesn't matter where you start on the color wheel; just pick a color to start with, and work clockwise or counterclockwise all the way around until you arrive at your starting point. My wool display starts with yellow greens in the top left corner and works its way across, transitioning into the cooler greens; the second level starts with blues and continues through purples; the third tier is full of reds and rusts; and finally, the fourth tier holds the golds and neutrals.

Storage Solutions for Small Pieces

It is easy to store equal sizes of fabrics. You fold them neatly and stack them, right?

Well, the real challenge is knowing what to do with odds and ends from previous projects that don't necessarily conform to the masses. As a group, they are unruly and nonconforming.

Some years ago, I was faced with this storage problem of an ever-increasing volume of leftover oddments from assembling kits. I loved having this stash of pieces to resource from, but things were getting a little problematic every time I needed to cull from it. It required dumping out the wool, scrambling to find a suitable color, then returning everything to the box.

If I had to total up the time I spent digging through my scrap boxes (yes, there were more than a few sizeable boxes), I could have probably hooked a few more rugs. So I got busy pondering the possibilities of organization, and I came upon a solution at a well-known Swedish furnishing store that I thought would work perfectly—and it has. See-through stackable storage bins now keep everything perfectly organized and easily accessible.

The final storage dilemma we all face is what

to do with leftover strips. Initially, I stored them all in a plastic zippered food storage bag, until they became too numerous. When that happened, I moved them into a vinyl zippered bag from a set of sheets that I had just purchased. Well, that did not take too long to outgrow, so I switched to the larger vinyl zippered bags that comforters come in. It was storage evolution in the making.

When I outgrew that larger bag, the only solution that remained was to begin separating the strips into smaller portions. The most logical idea that came to mind was to separate by color.

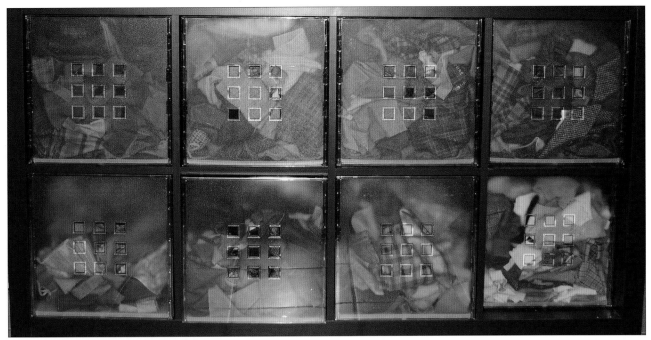

An eight-cube storage unit with 12" high x 12" wide x 14" deep clear plastic drawers is ideal for storing odd-sized pieces.

I now have a separate bag for each of the following colors: red, rust, gold, yellow greens, blue greens, blue, and purple. As providence would have it, my new storage system became the perfect setup to begin my forays into scrappy rug hooking. I now have my strips stored in purchased vinyl zippered bags (equal in size) that I purchased online, and the bags are now standing like books on a shelf with the colors showing through for easy access. Heaven knows what the next step will be, or if there will be another one, but my present storage of all those wild and woolly strips is working well for me now.

Making It Work for You

With everything in its place, my process for the inevitable wool hunt goes something like this. When I am in the process of color planning, I use full quarter-yard pieces since the larger the piece, the better I can appreciate how it will relate to other colors. But once the color plan is decided on, I set the quarter-yard pieces aside and search through the scrap pieces to find exact and close matches, as well as colors that will blend and add interest to the color field. As I begin the hooking process, I bring out the strip bags so I can add worms into the scraps or

Vinyl bags keep red, rust, gold, yellow greens, blue greens, blue, and purple strips in line.

THE VALUE OF VALUES

The muted, jewel-tone, and bright palettes shown in this photo have been selected to reflect the colors in medium value ranges. These medium values of colors usually display the best characteristics of color—the emotive qualities—and we find ourselves drawn by this call. Because we see the emotive qualities of the color in the medium ranges most clearly with the naked eye, we tend to purchase more wool in this range than any other.

In my preparations for writing this book, I had the privilege of looking at many rug hookers' stashes in their homes and saw this principle bear out in what most people purchased or dyed. Without sounding too much like an overbearing saleswoman (I hope), I like to encourage rug hookers to select at least three values of one color to add to their collection. When attempting to distribute color in a balanced way throughout the rug, using a different value will add more interest and keep rugs from looking flat.

Take a look at your stash. See if your collection of wools bears out this "medium value dominance" theory of mine. If so, pick out a few of your favorite pieces, take them with you when you go shopping next, and choose some pieces that will be darker and lighter variations of those colors. You will be delighted when you add them to the stacks on your wool shelves and see how quickly they bring depth and interest. Imagine what they will do for your rugs!

Visual samples of three color palettes: muted (top), jewel tones (middle), and brights (bottom).

quarter-yard pieces. Since the key to utilizing scraps is to mix them in with many other woolens, those scraps are part of the process for every rug I make.

All my wool is in constant rotation. My rugs have become like a veritable soup pot of pieces from past and present wool supplies. Yes, begin to think of your rugs as a humble pot of soup, okay? In the end, your rugs will be as individual as you are, blending all the variables at your disposal and filled with the complexities of a myriad of colors, shades, and tones. Sounds good, doesn't it? Organization will help to bring this about.

Of course, other methods for organizing all of the assortments of wool are out there. Some of the methods I have seen are strips of varying sizes pinned to brass rings. If you have one ring for each of the primary (red, yellow, blue) and secondary (orange, green, purple) colors, that would take this system a step up the organizational ladder. Clear plastic shoeboxes

make excellent containers for leftover strips, too. Another method I have seen is the bundling of like colors of strips tied together with selvedge. The ease of this lends itself to just pulling out a strip from the bunch. Perhaps these bunches can be stored with their companion strips in the vinyl zippered bags. That would cut out one step in the search process, and with all the time that rug making requires, you really want to preserve precious time for hooking.

You will be surprised at how much of what you have can be put to work in your rugs, but the key to utilizing as much as possible is truly adopting a method of accessibility and order. The great reward to all of this investment of thought and time will reveal itself immediately in your hooking life, and in the chapters ahead, you will come to appreciate the depth and interest that will develop in your rugs. That, in itself, is a reward all its own.

KNOW YOUR PALETTE

On the first day of a workshop I am excited and ready to go and would rather forgo the preliminaries like introductions, agenda, and so on. I want to see what everyone has brought along. Each student shows up with his or her own array of samplings from collections at home, and from them, I get a taste for each individual's preferences, not just for colors but for general palettes as well. Almost everyone shows up with a bit of samplings from all kinds of palettes—be it muted and primitive, jewel toned, or bright—showing evidence of his or her hooking history in leftover fragments of past rugs accomplished. The wool pieces hang collectively on a brass ring or sometimes tussled in a bag, begging to become a part of the process. The groupings may have a few pieces that are out of color character, but from a quick look, I can immediately establish a predominant working palette of the owner.

Most of us work across the spectrum of diversified palettes. We choose our colors by emotive qualities that are inherent in pattern designs. However, many confine their work to identifiable tones, like those who favor primitive design and color, for example. Whatever your predilection, remember that color theories that influence good composition and balance remain constant with all palettes and include a good range of values (light, medium, and dark).

THE COLOR YELLOW

An interesting fact about the color yellow is that it truly is incapable of becoming dark. Ever hear of anyone calling yellow "dark"? Sadly, or perhaps gladly, yellow will never be able to match the depth of the other primary colors without losing its identity. Its inherent light nature makes it very useful in creating contrast with black. We commonly find the yellow and black color combination in signage because of the strong contrast that is created by the two colors. You cannot darken yellow by the addition of more yellow. You might want to "darken" it by the addition of browns or orange, but it then loses its identity and moves into the realms of gold or brown.

Chapter 2

Color Blending to Extend Wool

Summer Winds, *detail (see the full rug on page 112). Summer Winds is an example of learning when to create contrast and when to blend. In the green sepal of the flower are many varieties of green. By name, see if you can pick out the olive, mint, aquamarine, sage, light chartreuse, kelly, and khaki greens.*

T his, in a nutshell, is the summary of my stylistic concerns: I have a love for color and contrast and like every motif to be identifiable against the background in any given format.

However—and there's usually a however—I do work to blend color within the motif parts as shown in the close-up of the scalloped flower in *Summer Winds*. This rug is the culmination of many lessons learned over the years, but one of the more important lessons is to know when to blend and when to create contrast. My preferred style is to create a strong foundation of contrast with a very dark or very light background so I have the opportunity to blend a larger range of middle values within the motifs.

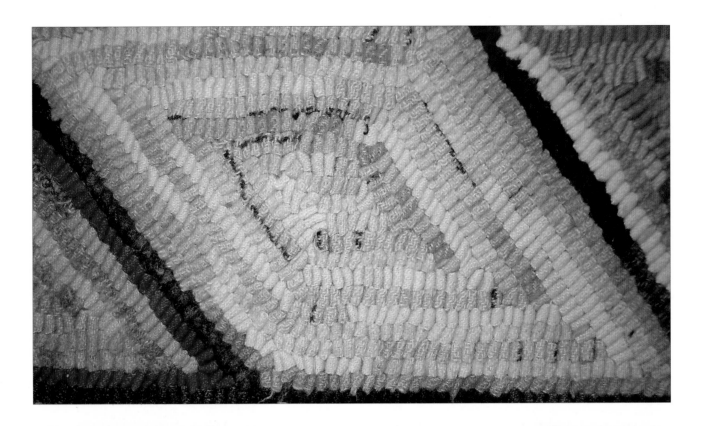

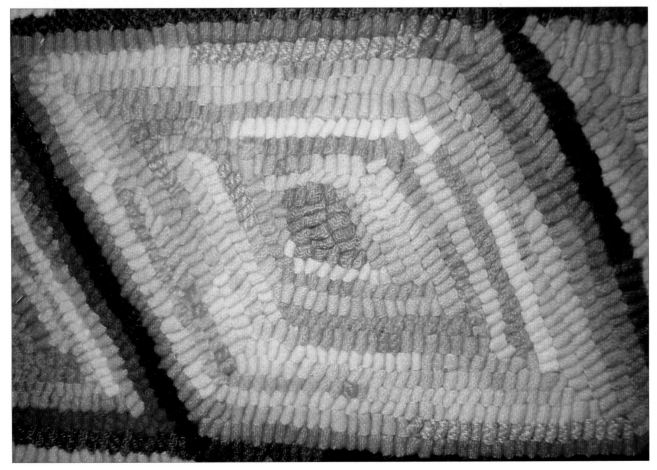

Wonky Diamonds, *detail (see the full rug on page 88). The top and bottom diamonds use many of the same woolens. The diamond on the top has darker values in higher proportion, whereas the diamond on the bottom features fewer darks with more highlights of very light values to give it a lighter and somewhat bluer cast.*

This display of wool samples shows the olive to turquoise spectrum, which occurs when blue is added to green in ever-increasing increments.

AN INTRODUCTION TO BLENDING

Since my early days of rug hooking, I have been fascinated with using many pieces of wool in a given area that are just slightly different in value and tone. In approaching a rug this way, I work with a curiosity about just what are the boundaries of mixing wool colors that keep a shape or area cohesive and how far can I push the boundaries without threatening the "color read" of that particular area or motif. It is a tension that I love, and I have come upon some discoveries of just how a colored area can change in its readability by the injection of colors that are just a little different.

As an example, I have isolated two different areas from my rug *Wonky Diamonds* that demonstrate many of the same wools being used; however, with the inclusion of lighter tones plus the more aqua tones, the diamond on the bottom reads lighter and cooler. It is still

CHECK YOUR TEMPERATURE

Many teachers use the words "warm" and "cool" to describe colors. A good way to remember these terms' definitions is by association of warm with the sun's colors, which we commonly recognize as reds, oranges, and yellows. On the other hand, think of cool by associating it with water's colors, which are commonly green and blue.

If an instructor should say that the red you are using is a "cool red," it is not an oxymoron. In its dominant state, the color is identifiably a red, but if it veers toward the maroon, it has been influenced by blue dyes, which give it a tendency toward the cool, albeit still red, color.

light olive or muted chartreuse in its dominant nature (which is decidedly warm), but the higher proportion of the lights and aqua strips render it subtly different.

Since we are in the green family, let's take a look back at the color wheel made of wool pieces on page 5. If we begin by seeing that the green family exists between the blue and yellow, we can also note that although a dominant influence of either blue or yellow may be a characteristic of a green, it still sustains its membership in the green family. With all its variations, I think green is a good starting place to begin to see how a good amount of blending from its broad range of tones will not affect its identity in the green family.

First, let's take a look at green from its origins in the yellow family and how, with increasing additions of blue, it moves toward the opposite end of the green spectrum (blue) yet still keeps within the boundaries of its identity. Starting out with characteristics of chartreuse, imagine increasing the addition of blue and you will begin to witness green's progression across the spectrum until it becomes associated with teal and turquoise tones.

In the scope of the infinite, I have selected a few examples of colors that were blended to demonstrate not only the blending abilities of close values but also how moving across the spectrum of the woolens displayed can influence the shift of a color's identity.

Blendable Colors

The examples of color play on this spread are but two in a myriad of possibilities when you consider all the colors the universe has to offer. Given some time, thought, and observation, there is a strong likelihood that you will find plenty of blendable colors in your stash. If you have at least three or four colors that will blend, you can easily double or triple the space that one color might fill alone. If you can create a spectrum of transitioning color they could easily form the basis of a good color plan.

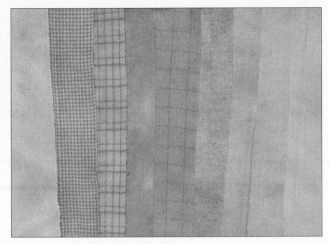

Turquoise to grasshopper green spectrum.

Turquoise to Grasshopper Green Spectrum

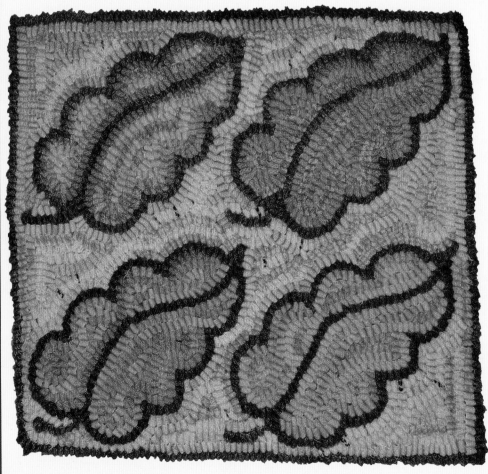

Leaf Sampler: *Turquoise to grasshopper green spectrum.*

This sampler employs a turquoise to grasshopper green spectrum to demonstrate the possibility of altering color by the insertion of progressively yellower tones of wool. Beginning with the brightest blue on the left, I hooked the leaf in the top left corner with the first four samples in the photo. For the second leaf, I dropped the first two blues on the left and picked up the next two (fifth and sixth from left). I continued dropping the first two from the left and picking up the next two to the right until the last leaf (lower right corner) was hooked using the last four colors in the spectrum. All of the leaves are outlined in the same khaki brown.

Red to Gold Spectrum

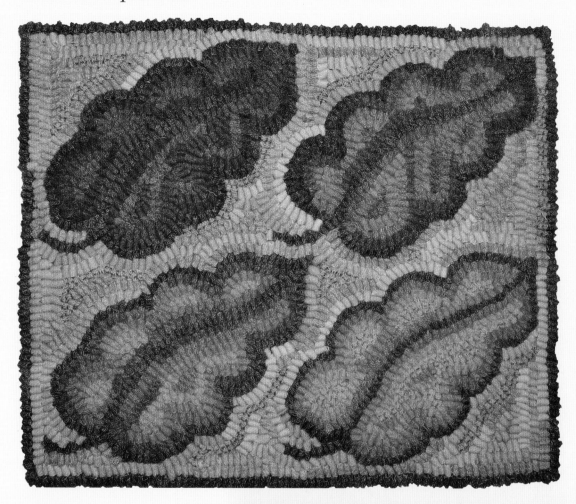

Leaf Sampler: *Red to gold spectrum.*

In this sampler, I used the red to gold spectrum to demonstrate the possibility of altering color by the insertion of progressively yellower tones of wool. Using the same technique, I started with the reddest color on the left and ended using the last four colors in the spectrum. All of the leaves are outlined in the same khaki brown.

Consider how either of these leaf samplers would be a more interesting alternative to a pattern with a spray of leaves that are just outlined and filled in with the same repeated wool color. The beauty of the transitional spectrum is that you can create variations that will transform the passing glance of a viewer to a close-up and intrigued inspection of all your varied and unique details.

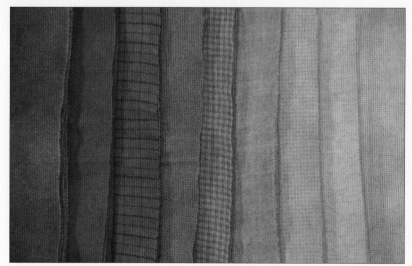

Red to gold spectrum.

The human eye has the capacity to identify more variations of green than any other color. It is believed that this capacity is built into the brain for survival purposes. You can well imagine the hunter-gatherer seeing from afar just the shade of green in a certain bush that provided him with luscious berries a few days prior in another part of the woods.

When choosing colors to blend, consider what is available to you in your stash within the full spectrum of a given color family. Experiment with shifts of value within this spectrum as well. As shown in the *Summer Winds* detail (see page 10), change-ups in the value give each strip row a distinction, but because they are within the same color family and close in value— along with the strong, deep background color providing a healthy dose of contrast—the shape of the sepal retains clear readability.

Funky Southwest, Calliope, Wonky Diamonds, and *Talavera I* show some terrific uses of color blending from among the rugs in the Gallery Walk. Look at each one closely and examine the variations of a single color family that make it the readable color that it is. Consider those colors and what is in your stash that might replicate those mixes in your rugs. Be sure to not overlook your already cut strips to add just a dash of the unexpected that will pull the eye of the viewer in to see just how you got that fabulous mix.

Calliope, *detail (see the full rug on page 92).*

Funky Southwest, *detail (see the full rug on page 104).*

Wonky Diamonds, *detail (see the full rug on page 90).*

Talavera I, *detail (see the full rug on page 94).*

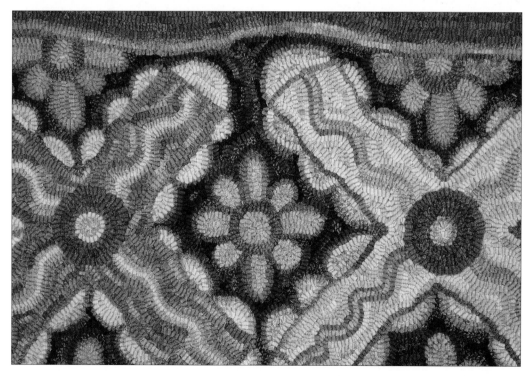

While there are many variations of color mixes in all of these examples, take note that the spectrum of choices within each color field varies by degree. Some are very close in value, showing a soft blending that nears a more solid look, with subtleties that can only be appreciated by closer inspection. Others use a wider range of tone and value that render the hooked area more textural in appearance. Given some thought, you may feel more connected to any one of these samplings above the others. If so, consider that a clue to something that lies inside you and may be begging to be expressed in a rug sometime soon.

WORKING WITH COMPLEMENTS

Choosing to work with complements can create startling results in your rug. If you are at a loss as to where to start, an examination of the color wheel will lead you to any of the following complementary color relationships.

Red and green. Think of joining the forces of these two complements by using every variation of red to include coral red, raspberry red, garnet, barn red, turkey red, and tomato red. In the green family be sure to include pine green, cactus green, olive green, sea foam green, and grass green. Open up the range for both of these color groups by moving into the analogous colors. For the red family, you can include red orange and red violet, and for the green family, you can include selections from the blue green and yellow green hues. Play around with different values and see what will work without breaking up the field and losing definition.

Yellow and violet. This complement set will probably send most people running, but it need not scare you away. In the yellow grouping, think of all the variations of golds that you have seen at your favorite vendor's booth. Think of the golds that are just barely kissed with a hint of green, brown, or rust. And for those who are just plain scared of purple, think of muted versions calmed with the hints of black or brown in their dye. Stretch yourself by moving into their neighboring color families, which will open up your options to the blue violet and red violet families along with the yellow greens and yellow oranges. These two groups might be a little more familiar by names like olive green, sage green, and muted chartreuse or melon, light coral, peach, and mango. Be mindful of values here, too, to keep your color fields united, or cast your cares to the wind and experiment with how many differing values your color field can handle.

Blue and orange. This complementary relationship is probably the most commonly used among rug hookers. I often see pumpkins surrounded by some kind of sky blue color. The most commonly used blue among us is the Williamsburg or Colonial blue that is slightly muted and in the middle range of values. When considering the full range of blues, begin with true blue that is likened to the sky in many rugs. Denim and chambray blues continue the progression and when a touch of green is added, the indigos come into play. Then come the peacock blues that in their lighter values are more reminiscent of aquamarine until reaching the turquoise blues.

When considering partnering the blues with orange, begin with the clearest of corals, then move toward orange peel. Darkening them with additions of black or brown will render them the shade of pumpkins and then finally to rust. Increasing the degree of additions of red will take them to the orange-red colors that are reminiscent of terra cotta (in lighter shades) to red jasper (in darker shades).

Chapter 3

Techniques for Scrappy Rugs

The nitty-gritty hooking techniques for scrappy rugs are the same as the hooking techniques for any hand-hooked rugs: insert hook into backing, pull up loop, repeat. However, there are a few techniques—or perhaps strategies—that relate especially well to working with the various and sometimes seemingly endless shades and tones that are common in scrappy rugs. Let's take a look at those here.

CREATING CONTRAST FOR DEFINITION

To say that I often juxtapose complementary colors in my rugs is a grave understatement! Inasmuch as the color wheel can overwhelm most of us with all the variables of color relationships, I use it in a very simplified manner. The use of complements is very simple in that all you have to do is draw a straight line across (diametrically across) the color wheel and the colors at each end will be complements. At the risk of dating myself, I am often reminded of all the effort that was expended in my childhood to avoid wearing colors that clashed or that were too loud. I can only chuckle now, because though my rugs have an identifiable color style, my focus throughout their construction is really all about exercising that formerly forbidden "clash."

Take another look at the color wheel on page 5, and notice how red is diametrically across from green. Other complements are simply orange and blue, purple and yellow.

I use the simplified names of these colors, but to work out more sophisticated versions of these color relationships, it helps to remember that we don't have to stick to the primal tones that we see on the color wheel. If I could draw in your imagination, think more in some of your favorite color names, like: cranberry and olive;

pumpkin and deep ocean blue; plum and gold. The main idea here is that if you are going to use the color wheel as a resource, don't get stuck in the colors presented in their printed form; it will point you to a mere hint of possible resolutions. The rest will be up to your mind to summon all the variables within a color family.

There can be no contrast without the use of extremes in values. I make sure that lights will hit against mediums and darks, and vice versa. I manage the varying degrees of contrast throughout the rug with balance, just as I would manage color. Working with lighter values of wool provides me with visual stimulation that can really come in handy when working with a particularly large rug. Every time I see a light color made lighter by the darker wool that is right next to it, it is like a shot of caffeine!

In an attempt to double my pleasure, I will often employ the use of complements while also doing a "switch-up" on the value of a complement. Bringing in a complementary light value against a medium or dark value will bring a glow factor to your overall composition as well as definition to the two areas that will be side by side on your rug. Remember to be mindful about using this technique in a balanced way, distributing your light, medium, and dark colors throughout your composition.

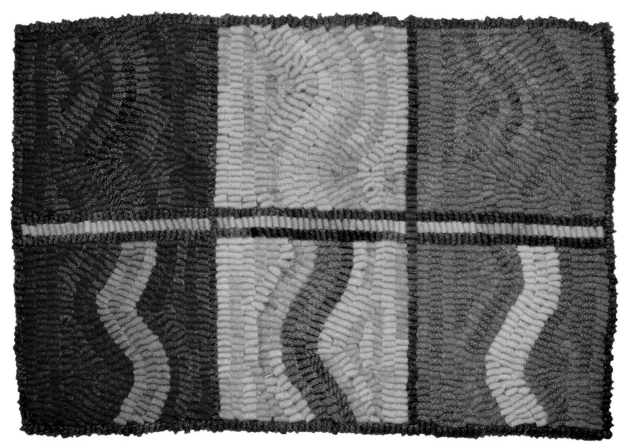

This sampler demonstrates the complement and switch-up technique by showing lighter and darker values of complementary colors together. Look at the bottom row of stripes where a greater shift in value occurs between the background and the stripe. The "pop" in the bottom row is evident.

Big Star, *detail (see the full rug on page 98).*

In the *Big Star* detail, the darker value of the orange family of colors heightens the luminosity of the lighter aquamarine. Imagine if the aquamarine were darker; the glow would be diminished.

In the *Jessica's Garden* detail, the fern is a combination of light chartreuse wools. Because this green has very strong yellow qualities, it functions like a direct complement to the dark plum background. Purples are often set against oranges and greens because both colors have a component of yellow, which is purple's true complement.

In the detail of *Diamond Trio*, the tiny aqua

Jessica's Garden, *detail (see the full rug on page 106).*

Diamond Trio, *detail (see the full rug on page 68).*

triangle gleams against the muted corals that surround it. In the lower left corner of the detail shot, notice the gold diamond set against the muted purple; the purple is darker, setting it up with a more subdued glow because of the gold's muted state.

The detail of *Talavera I* contains two incidences of complements. The larger is the X shape that is filled with a very yellow saturated green that is light in value with plum colored waves running through its center in a darker value. Then take note of the daisies in a mix from the orange family set upon a dark green background.

All of the examples utilize the strategy of light against dark and dark against light. Imagine how diminished their glow would be if all the colors were similar in value! The degree of contrast, like so many other components of style, is really an individual choice. When looking at other people's work, give thought to the degree of contrast and how it may speak to you. As you identify a specific level of contrast, are you impressed with it enough to want to recreate it for yourself? Also consider that contrast is just

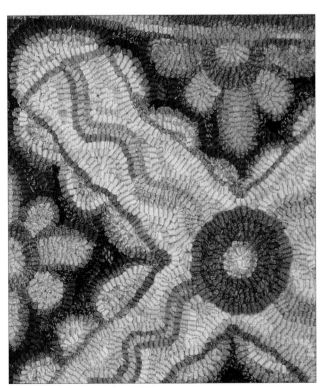

Talavera I, *detail (see the full rug on page 94).*

another element that can be employed by degree. And as with all other components of art, it is just one other tool to put in your arsenal of developing style.

Three Flowers, *27" x 10½", wool on linen. Designed and hooked by Bea Brock.*

Three Flowers, *detail showing third tile.*

USING OUTLINES

Of all the techniques used in rug hooking, outlining is the most common. It is a great tool in that outlining functions in so many ways that are not always appreciated. For example, outlining does all of the following:

- Adds detail to a shape when done in a complementary or lighter color
- Distributes color throughout a design by pulling color from one area of design into another
- Brings definition to a shape, keeping it from getting too bulbous
- Helps to extend the use of wool by reducing the area needing to be filled

A Study in Outlining

I got curious about the prospect of adding progressive details with outlining and how that could bring life to a design. My results of working out the progression visually explain the dynamic that a simple outline can bring to your work.

The first tile at the top of page 24 is hooked straight forward with single wool filling, the second is hooked with contrasted outline and solid fill, and the third is hooked with a combination of contrasted outlining, blended fill areas, and beaded outlining. The third example shows the most stylized dynamic of all three examples. It is not a judgment of good, better, best, but an example of what detailing can do to change the "feel" emanating from your work.

Inasmuch as a pattern can provide you with an inherent dynamic, you can then take that dynamic and expand on it to a degree that suits you and your personal interpretation of the design. Remembering that complexity pulls in the viewer's eye, you can modulate complexity as one of many components in your composition.

Summer Winds, *detail (see the full rug on page 112). A close-up shows the common outlining with differing values of bronzy olive.*

Using Neutrals to Outline

In most of my work, I use very little neutral coloring. I realize this trait is peculiar to my personal palette. Neutrals play more of a supporting role in the rugs I hook. I like to use them as a minor element by which colors will evidence themselves in a clearer way.

In *Summer Winds*, I used a bronze olive in varying values to play as an outline all across the composition. I previously used the word "minor" to describe my use of neutrals, but what it does is give the overall composition a toned-down effect in addition to giving the entire composition a more cohesive blend throughout.

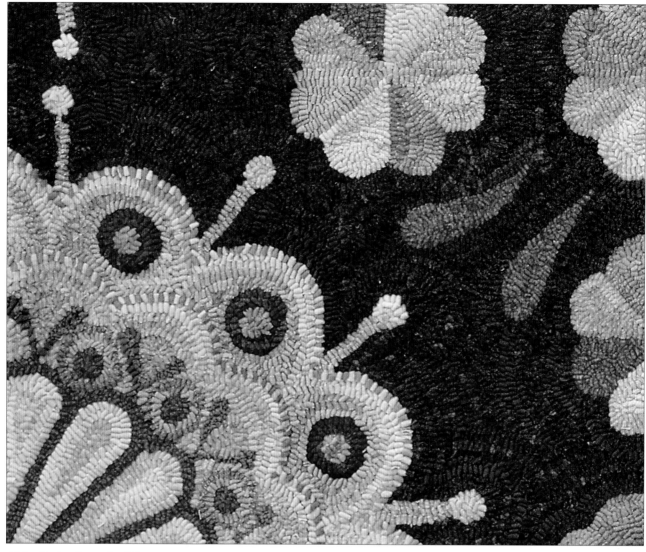

Abigail, *detail (see the full rug on page 108).*

Because of all the differing colors of each of the motifs, *Summer Winds* needed a unifying factor to pull it all together. So, yes, proportionately, the bronze olive was minor, but its contribution to the overall design was quite major. Granted, the impact of the color of the rug is the first thing that is communicated to the viewer, but on close inspection, the viewer is hopefully pleasantly surprised by the muted influence that the bronze olive outline lends to the vast array of colors used.

Let It Show

Since my preference for dark backgrounds remains constant for most of what I do, I keep in mind that I want my outline to be an integral part of the composition. For that reason, I make

sure that the outline is not so dark that it won't show up. This means that I will be juggling the value of the outline between the values of the dark background and whatever value fills any given shape.

If you have a preference for lighter backgrounds, you will have to move in a darker direction for outlining, but not so dark that it does not show up against your fill color. Look closely at the *Summer Winds* detail; you will notice varying values of that bronzy olive straddled in value between the two depths— that of the background and the motif, or whatever it sits between. To me, to lose an outline is to lose definition, which in turn will weaken your composition.

Color Pies, *detail (see the full rug on page 76).*

Use a Fill Color

Another option is to outline with a color that is being used as a fill color elsewhere in the design. Thistechnique will work in an effort to distribute colors throughout the design and bring cohesiveness to your work.

In the detail of *Abigail*, similar colors were used to outline the corner wedges and in the two sets of wedged circles. The light gold that is filling the wedges encores on the scallop's outline. Then of course, they are both repeated in the Dresden motifs in the center for the grand finale (see the full rug on page 108).

The final example is in *Color Pies*, where the outlines are also fill colors in other parts of the rug. The strategy is more random in impression, but nevertheless, it works the same way to distribute color throughout the design.

Wonky Diamonds, *detail (see the full rug on page 88). Double outlining can add a new dimension to a scrappy rug.*

Double Outlining

Another option available to you is double outlining. In *Wonky Diamonds*, the pattern is predictably repetitive. To engage the viewer's eye, double outlining was used.

Shown are two details of different versions of

this pattern, each with its own variation on the double outline. The first version shows the brown outline running throughout the pattern with a contrasting inner outline that is a complement to the fill color. In the second version, Martha Reynolds stayed within the

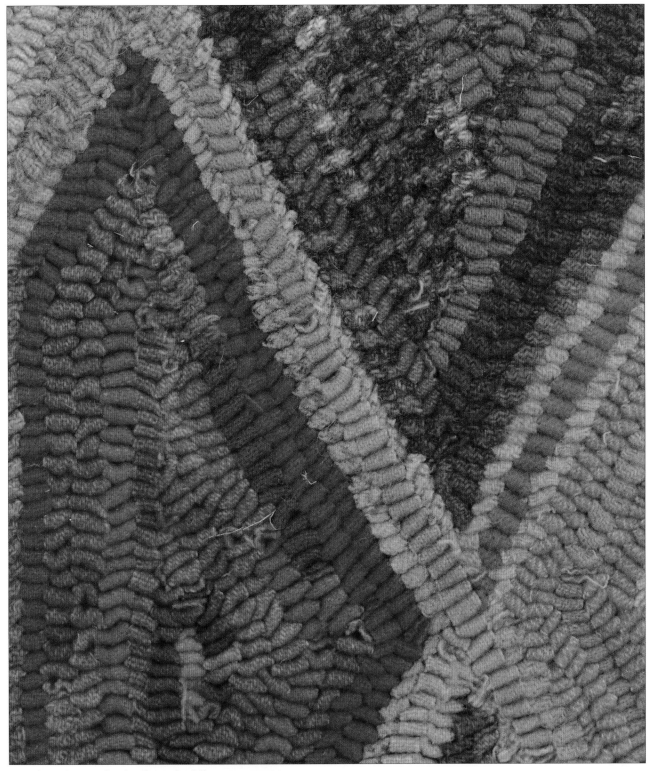

Wonky Diamonds, *detail (see the full rug on page 90).*

same color family of gold and created added interest by the shifting of values that randomly occur throughout the rug.

Try using two different colors on the outline, and you will see that it adds a new design element to the shape being hooked. It can re-

duce the size of the shape and require less of one main color, which will help to stretch your wool overall. Oftentimes using this technique will also give a shape a slimmer look, as in a flower petal that would have otherwise appeared heavy and bulbous.

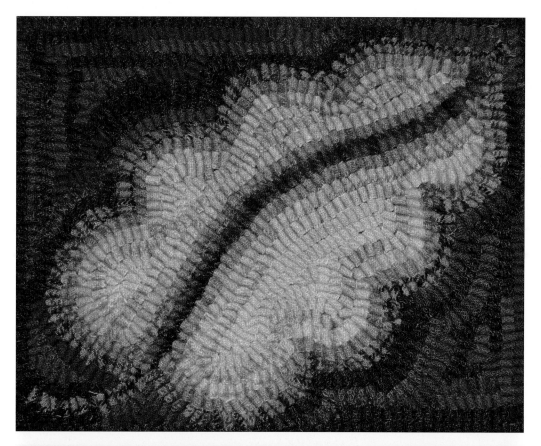

Leaf Sampler, *detail of concentric rows (see the full rug on page 14). The rows in this close-up shot are hooked concentrically within each half of the leaf shape.*

Leaf Sampler, *detail of vein accents (see the full rug on page 14). Here the leaf is accentuated by veins, which give it a reliable diagonal energy.*

HOOKING DIRECTION

When our learning becomes so ingrained, we often proceed as usual, giving little mind to possibilities. Hooking direction is one of those things that has become subject to the routine, and we seldom give thought to doing things any differently than we have before. Consider the squiggly lines that we commonly put in our backgrounds or the straight-across rows in our borders. Hooking direction is just another decision in the aesthetic construction of our rugs. To the left are two examples of the subtle contributions that hooking direction can make in the final outcome. These examples are by no means exhaustive, but once again, a few possibilities in the realm of the infinite.

The leaf on the top is hooked concentrically within each half of the leaf shape. The shift in value along the edge gives it a soft vibration, but if we have to gauge where it falls in the spectrum of static to energetic, I would give it a 3 out of 10 rating (on a scale of 1 to 10).

The leaf on the bottom is accentuated by veins, which give it that reliable diagonal energy and more forward movement than the leaf on the top. I might give it a 4 or 5 on the energy scale, although it is a subtle progression.

The importance of hooking direction is not to be underestimated. It adds significant qualities to overall movement. The artistic qualities of the final composition rely on the movement working in tandem with all other components like color, value, balance, and so on. Like all the other factors, it is an element of style that will provide its contribution to your personal expression.

Chapter 4

Working with Patterns and Designing Your Own

A FIRM FOUNDATION: STARTING WITH A PATTERN

Patterns fill the rug hooking market with many options to consider. If you are not at a place where designing your own pattern is a viable option, you'll need to consider several things if using up your current stash is your goal. We'll look at three ways that you can utilize your scraps, but each of them will depend on what your stash comprises. Some of us only buy wool for a specific rug. If your tendencies are to purchase for earmarked projects, you will probably have a lot of small pieces in a wide range of colors left over from previous projects. And if you have been hooking a long time you may have many variations of one color or more. Begin by sorting your colors into groups (see chapter 1) and ask yourself some questions.

Calliope, *detail (see the full rug on page 92).*

Do you have many variations (of green, for instance) that would add up to some sizeable yardage or at least to a quarter of a yard or more?

If you have a pretty sizeable stash with a lot of possibilities for blending (see chapter 2), you can consider patterns that have larger areas to fill. A case in point is *Calliope,* hooked by Janet Griffith. Janet has been hooking rugs for nearly 20 years and has a sizeable stash. *Calliope* was a pattern that was suited to her collection in that she is an avid dyer and had many variations of the main colors to fill the spaces with slightly varying tones and shades of each color.

If you have a tendency to be drawn by certain colors, it is likely that you will have variations in tone that are particularly suited to blending. Smaller scraps, like the red, green, and amber in Janet's piece, will take care of the minor areas.

Take a good look at your stash and combine colors that will blend and extend the areas that they can fill. Thereafter, look for groups that will vary in value so you can think of them in terms of what color they will look good next to. Tearing

larger pieces of wool into measureable strips that mimic leftovers cut from a quarter yard will be helpful. A washed quarter yard will measure about 16" long and 27" wide. Place all the strips that you expect to use side by side in an area of that size to approximate a quarter yard.

Do you have a near-overwhelming amount of smaller scraps?

Perhaps you have been rug hooking for a number of years and your scraps are growing by leaps and bounds. You have strips left over from projects, odd pieces from your recycle wool days, and many, many small pieces less than 4" or 5" wide. A pattern to eat away at this ever-growing collection of tidbits will require a unique design.

If this description fits you, a pattern designed for repetitious shapes that doesn't require a repetitious color plan will put a dent in your stash. *Color Pies* was designed just for such a job, and my single challenge in executing it was to make sure that every color showed up well against its neighbor.

Like *Color Pies, Gumball Track* was designed for maximum color display, and Gina Paschal was able to put a serious dent in her scrap bag by the time she was done. Her collection was varied in color, but it was full of pieces and oddments that worked well together because her personal palette was all moderately muted or jewel toned. If you have confidence in your color likes, you will find that your scraps can all work together if you choose the right pattern to display the greatest variations of color.

Are your strips taking over your stash?

If your strips are beginning to overtake your wool collection, look for patterns that have simple motifs in the foreground and consider using the hit and miss strategy in the background. If your motifs are large and open, you can fill the spaces with wonderful stretches of strips that play light against dark. You can also

MEASURING WOOL

Measuring for the amount of wool needed is a very necessary skill for the rug hooker. Of course, not everything is a perfect square or rectangle, but between those two shapes and a triangle, you will be able to measure most motifs.

I generally square off motifs and multiply the area (length by width) times 6. For triangular shapes, I measure two sides (length and width), divide by 2, then multiply by 6. This factor of 6 covers for average hooking where there is no packing of the loops and the loops are not pulled up too high.

What is "too high," and what is "packing"? The general rule of thumb is to pull up a loop as high as a strip is wide. For example, for a #8 cut, pull your loops up $1/4$" high. Most of us, however, pull up loops at a consistent height that is common with our most frequently used strip size. Muscle memory takes over in that respect. Packing is pulling up loops very close together, which causes them to lose their rounded crown and become more folded than looped.

These characteristics of high and packed loops are exercised in varying degrees, but most who have these tendencies know who they are and can use the method below to calculate their wool consumption rate to measure for any given motif or project.

To find out how much wool you personally require, take a premeasured strip (in this case we will use a 15" one) and hook it in a straight line as you normally would. When you have hooked it all, measure the finished length. If you hooked a row measuring 2" long, divide 15" by 2 for $7\frac{1}{2}$". Therefore, when you measure an area, multiply the area by $7\frac{1}{2}$ to give you a more accurate amount. To err on the side of generosity, multiply by 8.

take a silhouette of a cat or dog, for instance, and work concentrically around the shape or create vertical or horizontal striping. Think of using hit and miss in borders or anywhere a stretch of straight hooking is called for. The border on *Gumball Track* (see the full rug on page 66) was a perfect solution to finish off the multi-colored motifs. The *Diamond Trio* rugs (see pages 62 and 68) offer perfect examples of a more controlled hit and miss technique. Each is a reflection of the hooker deciding what to use from her stash.

Take a look and see what you have going in your wool closet. Your assessments can lead you to clues on how to choose your pattern. And if you are brave, maybe you might want to consider designing your very own!

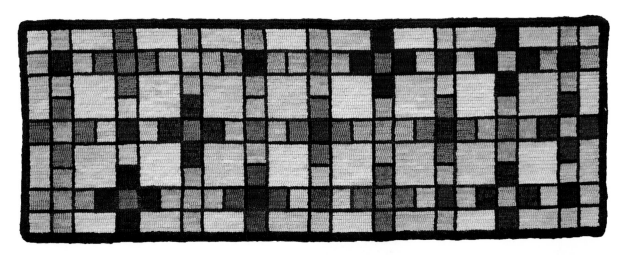

DABBLING WITH DESIGN: CREATING YOUR OWN PATTERN

I love to encourage rug hookers to design their own rugs. Despite meeting with reluctance from the masses, it is an important goal in my teaching. Many rug hookers seem overwhelmed by their lack of experience and don't even consider the prospect of designing, but as you will see, many avenues are available to the novice in the realm of geometric patterns combined with repetition.

Simply Square

Beginning with the simplest of elements, a straight line, we can come up with simple grids that beg to be filled with a spectrum of colors. The next step in thinking when dealing with simple grids is how to fill in the squares. Therein lays the opportunity for patterning that can utilize umpteen different colors in any number of ways. Consider the options in the designs in the following photos, and you will quickly see that the format truly lends itself to many possibilities.

The design for *Gridded Crosses* is as simple as you can get. And the delight of simplicity is that it leaves the gate wide open about how it will be filled with color. Other options in color play might be to alternate the cross colors and centers all across the format. Or how about repeating the two colors in a cross diagonally? The larger squares could also be another object of color attention. Consider the outcome if those larger squares were alternating with another light color or colors.

Gridded Crosses, *above, detail below.*

Square in a Square, *detail (see the full rug on page 84).*

Take a lesson from our quilting sisters and turn a square "on point." If you take the humble grid and set it on a diagonal, you have diamonds to work with. The dynamic of a diagonal line is not to be overlooked. The diagonal brings movement to a composition. When viewing strong diagonal statements our eyes glide across the format encompassing all sides of the composition's parameters. If our eyes gets stuck in one predominant area of the format, sweeping diagonals may be the cure to get the eye moving all across the plane.

Square in a Square has two dynamics going, all created from straight line drawing. Because the squares were created by diagonal lines, the design contains the movement that is inherent in this directional quality. Also, the varied sizes of squares within create another dynamic of scale. These same qualities are repeated in the simple *Half Cabin* design.

Straight edge designs need not be boring or tedious. The fun in designing with straight lines is that the designs can be easily accomplished with paper, pencil, and a ruler. Or you can do it freehand, like *Wonky Diamonds*, shown earlier, and not give a care to its lack of engineering. Some of the most fun rugs I have hooked have been designed with a very loose hand, not caring about perfection. It allowed me to indulge my color appetite with great abandon.

Half Cabin, *detail (see the full rug on page 110).*

UNDERSTANDING SCALE

An important facet of good design is scale. When our eyes meet a design in which all the motifs are the same size, our brains register it as predictable and static. If, however, we are viewing a composition that has variations in scale, our brains become a bit more intrigued.

Imagine a simple white tiled surface, 10' by 12', where all tiles are equally 4" square. It is predictable, and our minds find rest in it. We are not compelled to study or linger our gaze upon it. By contrast, still staying with white tiles, imagine a myriad of sizes of square tiles measuring from 1" square to 10" square over the same surface. We might be more inclined to look longer at the latter composition owing to its use of scale to draw in and hold the viewer's eye. It is not just how big or small something is that makes it interesting; it's the variations of size within a composition that make it a bit more attractive and intriguing to the viewer.

SAY "DEATH!" TO THE INNER CRITIC

In the middle of this discussion of pattern designing, it is necessary to bring up the subject of keeping a sketchbook. When I encourage my students to do this in my workshops, I do so with a mild trepidation. I know that in so many of our minds we do not see ourselves as artists and keeping a sketchbook is relegated to the practices of an artist and is not a privilege or practice to be exercised by the common. I am speculating here, but upon the very second we might entertain the idea of drawing or doodling in a book, we freeze at the thought of what might be recorded there: the good, the bad, and the ugly. This was my experience some years ago, but I told myself quite consciously that this blank sketchbook opened before me with its white intimidating pages was a "no critic zone." Once these pages were opened, the voices of past failures and unrealized expectations were not welcomed here. This was going to be a place where the fullness of who I am—without the doubts and ambivalences, no matter how they originated—was going to reign supreme in all of its graphic glory.

I took the plunge and made a solemn commitment to silence any critical mental whisperings that might stand as an obstruction to this honest exploration. It was going to be a visual sounding board to what I was, what I liked, and what I could concoct. I began by copying what I liked in magazines, books, fabrics, or whatever I encountered that intrigued me. It began as a recording of "likes." In the process, I began to tweak what I was seeing and recording and eventually transitioned after about a year's time into what I considered an original style. My sketchbooks are riddled with less than inspiring doodles, and I have accustomed myself to just turn the page over and forget about them. I do not make any assessments of what has transpired in my sketchbooks until it comes time to design. And then, the sketchbooks work as a resource from which to cull motifs that have possibility for rug patterns. I have filled about six or seven books in about eight years' time, and I enjoy seeing what is recorded there.

All this is to say that if you have a curiosity about the design possibilities within you, there is no way around it. To take the leap, silence the inner critic, inhale and muster the courage within, and begin your journey with the first steps of doodling in a sketchbook. The first page is always the most trying, but once you have gotten past the first page, the worst is over. Your books can keep anything in them. Keep recipes, grocery lists, daily reminders, phone numbers . . . anything to take the edge off performance anxieties.

Tell yourself it is not really a sketchbook—it's just an idea notebook. Use your time waiting in doctor's offices or appointment waiting rooms to fill it with the most casual of little line drawings. Develop the habit of running to your sketchbook whenever you have a passing idea that needs working out or one that needs addressing when you have more time available. Keep one with you at all times to have it ready at the helm, and you will be surprised how much can be done with a few minutes here and there. Soon you will have a wonderful resource to refer to for future projects, and rugs originating from it will be truly and completely your own.

An equally humble design element to consider is the use of stripes. Perhaps it may be too mundane to even consider doing a striped rug, but stripes are not necessarily relegated to longish lines all across the parameter. Consider breaking down shapes with stripes. If you have plenty of scraps that are a color plan in the waiting, think of patterning the colors with thick and thin stripes that play with varying degrees of contrast. To add a cohesive factor in a multicolored striped rug, outline your stripes with a single color outline.

Squares filled with alternating cool and warm stripes can be a great way to hone down your scrap pile. The traditional Log Cabin design is made up of concentric stripes. Or how about dividing your square in half along the diagonal, and you'll have what is known in quilting circles as Half Square Triangles. You can fill them with stripes that are concentric or do a warm and cool alternating pattern or a light and dark alternating pattern with them, too. Taking just those few simple elements—the square, the diagonal, and stripes—you can have any number of design options to move toward.

Each of these elements can be used in creating a good composition. It goes without saying that thought and planning are necessary

Color Pies, *detail (see the full rug on page 76).*

if you want to ensure a pleasing outcome. When we take any of the elements identified above and begin to consciously appreciate them in other good works of art, like paintings, prints, commercial fabrics, or print media, then they become tools we retrieve when we design our own works of art.

Going Around in Circles

One of my earliest fascinations in design was the circle. When I would sometimes come up blank and had some doodling time to spend, I would inadvertently go to the circle. I would begin to break it up into pie wedges then begin to embellish the sides of the wedge. My sketchbooks are filled with a lot of experimentation of this nature because it was my default design direction. No sooner would I finish a round motif than I thought about how I really should have done it; so, off I went to show how it really should have been done in the first place. But as soon as I got that done, I would have a curiosity about another version that popped into my head, and off I went again. An hour later, five or six versions—some inspiring, some less so— would be on the pages of my sketchbook. A few years later, I am wondering how many versions I came up with in total. I suspect at least 100

Posies in a Row, *detail (see the full rug on page 70).*

like, stick with concentric circles, like targets, but play with the concentric circles not being so equidistant. If you do like the idea of spokes emanating from the center circle, embellish those spokes. Turn them into a compass design with angled lines from its outer points toward the center circle.

These are just a few of the multitude of possible variations. Design as many variations as you can on this circle theme in a week's time, and you will have some wonderful resources to choose from for your next rug design.

After you have selected one or more motifs from what you have created, your next consideration will be how to arrange them within the format of your rug. Do you want them all spaced equally apart? Or do you want them nudged up right against each other? Will they all be the same size?

Consider the dynamic of scale previously discussed. Use your printer at home to enlarge or decrease the size of your motif, and see how it will fit with other motifs within the format.

All of these ideas can be worked out on paper before committing to your backing. When you feel you have come to a final composition in pencil, going over all the line work with a black marker will help you see if it is truly ready to be transferred to your backing.

Cut It Out, Tape It Down

If I have been successful in establishing a penchant for circular motifs in your design vocabulary, here is a throwback to your grade school days that is really quite fun and inexpensive. I bought a ream of 11" by 17" copy paper at my office supply retailer and keep it handy because its size is less restrictive for designing than an 8½" by 11". If you have freezer paper on a roll, that will work too. Teacher supply stores and art supply stores offer paper on rolls that is really handy to have around for projects like rug designing.

variations in the past two to three years, maybe more.

Here is how to begin. Draw a circle. It doesn't have to be a perfect one, as long as it reads like a circle. Find the middle point, approximately, and draw another circle inside the big circle. Now you have concentric circles. From here you can go a number of ways. The spokes of a wheel can originate from the center circle and you can embellish them with a dot at the end. Or if you

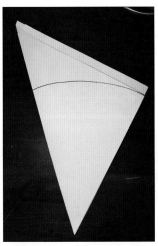

Fold to create eight sections.

Leave much of both sides connected.

Cut out the design.

Unfold the design and lay it on black wool.

Cut out the largest square or circle possible. For this example, I will use a circle cut from freezer paper. You can draw your circle with a pin, string, and pencil. Cut out the circle, then fold it in half, then in half again. One more fold and you can opt for a repeat of 8.

To begin drawing your design, remember that only the top edge will be cut from one end to the other on the wedge. All other designs can be cut from the right or left side but must not go across to the opposite end or you will cut off any portions beneath that line. I am right handed and prefer to cut from the right, and I will assume that left-handed people will prefer cutting from the left.

ASK AND RECEIVE

I was getting enlargements of some new pattern designs at a local graphics reproduction shop when the shop owner was complaining about how some large rolls of paper that he uses on his 36" copier were damaged by the shipper. The box of four rolls had sat in moisture that eventually leaked through the boxes. Though the damage was minimal, the shop owner did not want to attempt to feed the paper through his sensitive equipment for fear of creating paper jams. I offered to buy one of them if the price was reasonable and was pleased to hear that he would let me have them for $5 a roll.

Later, I learned that when he has a big blueprint job to do, he will often change a roll prematurely to avoid having to change rolls in the middle of a big copying job. So I asked how much for those. "Aw, nothing. Just take them with you. I'll be happy to get rid of them." My friends love me all the more for giving away these luscious rolls with five or six yards of paper on them. They are great for designing, and I use them often when making design adjustments to my existing master patterns. The paper is very white and a durable weight, and it is great for tracing. The next time you are at your copy store, ask if they have any extra rolls lying around that may be in need of a good home.

The designs should be simple. Remember that spaces within the lines of rug hooking motifs should be generous to allow for at least a couple rows of strips in your preferred cut. For instance, if you do a lot of hooking with a #8-cut strip, allowing ¾" of space for your design area will allow for three rows of loops. Repetition is considered pleasing to the eye in and of itself, so there is no need to get fancy here. Just place

Sample of design possibilities with cut paper motifs.

a few design lines here and there, and you will be amazed by the result.

To fully appreciate what you have created, carefully place your cutout on black construction paper, black foam core board, or a yard or more of black wool. If you have a dark stained dining table that would work, too. To print a copy, lay the paper design on a printer with a piece of black construction paper on top of it. Print one copy. I don't recommend using your printer at home for multiple copies because you will use up a tremendous amount of black ink in the process. Instead, run single original copies for reproduction at a copy shop. While you are there, consider reducing or enlarging some as well.

When you come home with those copies, play around with the arrangement of them. Will they be in a straight grid or staggered? Because we are dealing with round shapes, you may decide to have them all nudging up against each other with very little space between them. You may want to experiment with scale and add in some smaller versions as well.

If you decide on a grid formation, think about the space between the shapes. Is there room for smaller, different motifs in the center? If so, go back to the paper cutting method to come up with a shape that would complement the larger motifs. Perhaps an element from the larger motif could be simplified and repeated on a smaller scale. Just keep in mind the space for hooking that is necessary to finally execute the design. Once you have it all laid out, tape it together.

To get your design onto large white paper, measure the motifs and grid your large white paper with pencil marks to show where your motifs will fit in. Then, trace your motifs within the space allotted. There may be some miscalculations in the taping so be sure to adhere to the grid laid out on paper for more accurate positioning.

Border Security, or Lack Thereof

If you have played around with any of the design options, you have shown true pioneering spirit. You have worked hard and persevered thus far and now you might want to do a final assessment of whether you have reached a level of satisfaction with your design efforts. With the motifs now lined up and drawn on white paper, consider whether your design calls for a border. There are several aspects to think about in this decision.

Rug hookers harbor a general tendency to think that a border brings a finishing touch to all designs, so there is a natural inward push to get that border all around and bring the piece to conclusion. It is like having a wonderful photo that declares its need for framing. If you don't mind me slowing you down a bit, I would like to take you along on my evolving journey in thinking about borders.

HOW TO CHANGE A BORDER

In spite of all the patterns available on the market today, you may find one that suits all of your needs but have second thoughts about the border. You can envision some changes that you would like to make, but you are not sure how to go about doing it.

If portions of the motifs are repeated in the border, it will make for a continuity of design. The biggest dilemma you may face is how to repeat some of the motifs evenly in the border. The easiest way to measure is to take a piece of paper (or several pieces taped together) that replicates the border width and cut it to the length of the border. Decide on how many motifs—or portions of the main motifs—you may want to consider placing along the border. If you need to make an adjustment in the size of the motifs to better fit in the border, you will have to first trace them and then enlarge, or decrease them via your home printer or a copy shop. Next, fold the paper with enough folds to equal the number of motifs to be placed in the border. Each fold will mark the position where a motif will be centered in between. Trace your motifs onto the paper border strip and then lay the strip atop the pattern to see if it will work. If it does, slip the paper border under your pattern and use a marker to trace the motifs on the backing. If you are using monk's cloth or unbleached linen, you may have to use a window or light table to see the pattern underneath.

Early on when my pattern designs were strongly inspired by the primitive style, borders played a consistent part in my design process. As I moved along to a more personal style, I began to question whether that knee-jerk design reasoning was still serving me. Much of what I had designed in the past was very static in compositional style. Back then, the designs were simple motifs that replicated primitive themes with very little infusion of diagonal, gestural, or directional lines that would take the viewer's eye around the surface.

As my style evolved, curvilinear lines began to create energy and movement and I was faced with the consideration of whether a border would bring that energy to a screeching halt, or

Jessica's Garden, *detail (see the full rug on page 106).*

if I should let the design flow out to the edges and gently fade off the edge. The latter was something I had not previously considered. When I designed *Jessica's Garden* it was apparent that I did not want a border harnessing the energy or competing with it.

Oftentimes, a design that has energy and movement defies being constrained. In the past I have likened energetic design to a dance. This design dance can be vigorous or gentle, and sometimes constraining it within a border would be like trying to dance in a three-square-foot area bordered by a cinder block fence. Why not let the design float into the edges where it will come to a graceful stop?

The directional quality of *Jessica's Garden* is strongly outward and away from the center for the major motifs. On the other hand, the directional energy of *Summer Winds* is more circular. It reminds me of water spinning down a drain. There is but one major motif: the

scalloped flower that faces outward on two opposing diagonal corners. The rest of the motifs are swirling around the center motif. Because this movement is predominantly circular and inward, I used the scalloped border to contain it. The border contributes a quality of light containment for the overall composition.

So, give some consideration about whether a border really enhances the design. Assess how you feel about the energy present within the design. Is it energetic or static, or is its energy somewhere in between? Do you want to harness the energy or let it flow to the edges where it will gradually dissipate? If the design energy is static, do you want to bring some liveliness to it along the border? If you are working with a predesigned pattern, do you want to change it to suit your creative whims? Go with your decision even if it feels like it's against conventional rug hooking wisdom; you may enjoy the results!

COMMITTING TO COLOR PLANS ON PAPER

I have on occasion jumped right into hooking a rug with no preplan. I call that hooking on a wing and a prayer. The inevitable reverse hooking doesn't take long to show up soon after—along with uncertainty of artistic direction. Although I have a certain degree of patience for unhooking my work, I would just as soon avoid it if I can. I love the hooking process, the hours of sitting and covering the linen with countless colored loops. With that comes the deep satisfaction of productivity, especially after a full day of steady work. With experience, I have grown to cherish those feelings all the more, and because of that, I have taken to working out most of my color strategies ahead of time with colored pencil. In the case of the rugs that require more thought for balanced use of color, it has served me well and probably saved me countless headaches.

When working with an almost all-inclusive color palette, I often use a triangulation method of color planning. This is how it works. First, visually divide the design area into thirds. The object then is to have a color distributed throughout your composition in each of the three areas. Finally, imagine connecting the dots of those color positions so they make a triangle.

This method is particularly helpful for complex rugs in the absence of symmetry or repetition, but it will also work fine for repeated motif designs, too. Now, if you are thinking that you will have to move your linen and work on a separate third for every application of color, hold your horses. This is where color planning comes in. You can work it out on paper to make sure you have a good balance of color planned before you even begin hooking. Think back to your childhood days of crayons and coloring books. This method is quite doable and will save you hours of indecision that can all be worked out before a loop is even pulled.

Of course, you will have to get your pattern on paper. Take a photo of the pattern with your digital camera, and get a print of it through your printer. Make sure you shoot the photo straight up with all the sides running parallel to the camera's frame to minimize distortion in the final outcome. If the pattern is a little faint, go over it with a fine point marker to make the design more visible for tracing. Then trace the design to produce your first print on your printer. Enlarge your design so that it fills an 8½" x 11" piece of paper as much as possible.

Make copies of this tracing. You may want to lighten the lines to a light gray so that they are not a part of the colored design. With the pattern in light gray lines, you can color in your outline choice—if you have one—and it will not be competing with the black line that is really not a part of your design and may distract you from establishing good contrast by way of values.

Chapter 5

Finishing Scrappy Rugs

Topsy Turvy Chickens, *detail of wool strip bound edge (see the full rug on page 96).*

N ow that the end is in sight you have to keep your faculties under control. After all, you have spent considerable time getting all the other aspects of your rug just right; why not spend some thought on how you will be bringing this all to a grand finale?

My three preferred methods are yarn whipping without cording inserted into the fold of the binding, yarn whipping with cording inserted, and whipping with leftover strips and cording inserted. I tend to stick with these finishing techniques because they are textural in a way that complements the hooking. These firm edges protect the edge of hooking, and the yarn, if whipped moderately tight, will stand the test of wear on the floor. I will do variations on these methods that I think really bring some interest to the edge, as it is like choosing a frame for a great piece of art. How much better is a custom-made frame than a ready-made one?

One of my favorite things to do is to make the binding a continuation of the rug's design. I refer to it as "sacrificing for aesthetics" in that it does require collecting many colors of yarn for the binding to match the colors on the edge. But once the colors are collected, it requires no more time than a typical rolled binding. Slowing down the mental processes at the end of the project will reward you with an edging that required just as much aesthetic judgment as the rest of the rug.

Spring Has Sprung, *detail of matched binding on edge (see the full rug on page 102).*

PLAYFUL EDGY BINDING

Carrying colors along the edge into the binding is a method that has a way of incorporating the edged finish into the overall composition for design integrity. In *Topsy Turvy Chickens*, the edge is whipped with leftover strips from the rug and matched by color all along the edge. The textural quality of the strips offers an enhancement to the hooked texture and simplistic design motifs. Take notice of the blue separation line on the wavy border and how that color is brought in along the edge. It offers a surprise to the viewer and makes the edge an integral part of the design, not just a functional finish.

In the same vein of matching edges, *Spring Has Sprung* also carries color into the binding. When I finished the rug some years ago, I remember the feeling of wanting to have it done and be done with. Although I had in mind to match the edge, I knew that because there were so many different colors along the edge,

finishing it in this manner would prove to be a daunting task.

I heard distant inner whispers saying, "What's the hurry?" and was immediately calmed when I resolved to carry the strips of color with me at all times, and in particular when I was going to the yarn shop. I was able to match the colors pretty closely with what was available in needlepoint tapestry yarns. What I was unable to match, I dyed. It wasn't long before I had all the colors necessary to finish the binding.

Then I set upon the task, wondering if I was going to be able to tolerate changing yarn colors so often in the already tedious process of binding. A few seconds later, it occurred to me that I would not have to do so much switching if I just worked with one color at a time. So I began the process with one color; everywhere that one color appeared along the edge, I whipped it. Moving on, one color at a time, it did not take me long before the end was in sight.

I have to admit that it did take some resolve,

Dyeing Yarn

Despite my panic when the local yarn store went out of business some years ago, I am glad to have taken the plunge in yarn dyeing. If dyeing intrigues you, I would say it is slightly more complicated than warming soup on the stovetop. Here is what you will need: an electric skillet or kettle reserved for dyeing only, dye, measuring spoons, tongs or spoons, dye formulas, measuring cup, salt, and citric acid or vinegar.

1. 24" of worsted weight yarn will cover about 2½" of binding with a ³⁄₁₆" diameter cording. Measure your yarn by wrapping it around a 24" piece of cardboard with one complete wrap equaling 48" for every 5" of binding needed. Add five or six extra wraps.

2. While yarn is still wrapped around the cardboard, take four to six 8"–10" lengths of extra yarn or string and wrap figure eights around the wrapped skein, dividing it into three or four sections. Knot the string to itself, leaving the figure eights weaving loosely around the yarn. Do this throughout the skein in four to six evenly spaced places to minimize tangling while dyeing. Soak the yarn in warm water with a small amount of dishwashing detergent.

3. Heat water in the pot or skillet. Measure the formula in a measuring cup, dissolve it with hot water from the pot, and fill the measuring cup to 1 cup.

4. Pour 1 tablespoon of formula into the skillet or pot. Starting out the dyeing with 1 tablespoon of the formula is a precautionary method as most formulas are based on ½ yard lengths of wool fabric, which is approximately 6 ounces in weight. The yarn you will be dyeing is a small fraction of that, so if your initial outcome is too light, you can darken it incrementally until you reach your desired depth.

5. Add a skein to the dye bath, submerge it, and stir lightly. When the dye has largely been taken up and the water is almost clear, add 1 tablespoon of vinegar or ½ teaspoon of citric acid. Process for another 10 minutes, and remove the skein with tongs.

6. Let the skein cool. Submerge it in a cool water bath, taking care that the skein is not hit by running water. Remove the skein from the cool water, and squeeze out any excess water. If you have a lingerie bag, place the skein in the bag and spin it only by washing machine. Alternately, place the skein in a towel, roll it up, and squeeze out any excess water. Thereafter, hang the skein to air dry.

Detail of edge technique showing tri-toned binding to mimic multi-tonal background.

but in the end, my reward was that the rug had the finish I thought it deserved to bring out the best in the design.

The finish on *Talavera I* shows my first attempts at dyeing yarn. I had a favorite yarn store where they kept an expansive inventory of tapestry/needlepoint yarns in stock. They went out of business, and after my panic abated, I realized that my only alternative was to dye the wool myself. I read up on dyeing yarn, and the process seemed simple enough since I had already had many years of experience in dyeing wool fabric.

My first objective was to match the border edge in comparable value. Well, it didn't work out that way, and my first batch came out too dark. In my second attempt, it was a little on the light side. The fairy-tale ending was on the third try when the yarn came out just right. Then on went the proverbial lightbulb when I thought, "Why not use all three and it will mimic the mixed dark blue background?" A heathered yarn was born!

In *Diamond Trio*, Teena Mills used off-the-shelf variegated yarn skeins. One was a motley blue gray; the other, a motley rust red. She began whipping with the blue gray yarn for about 6". She wanted to incorporate the rust red

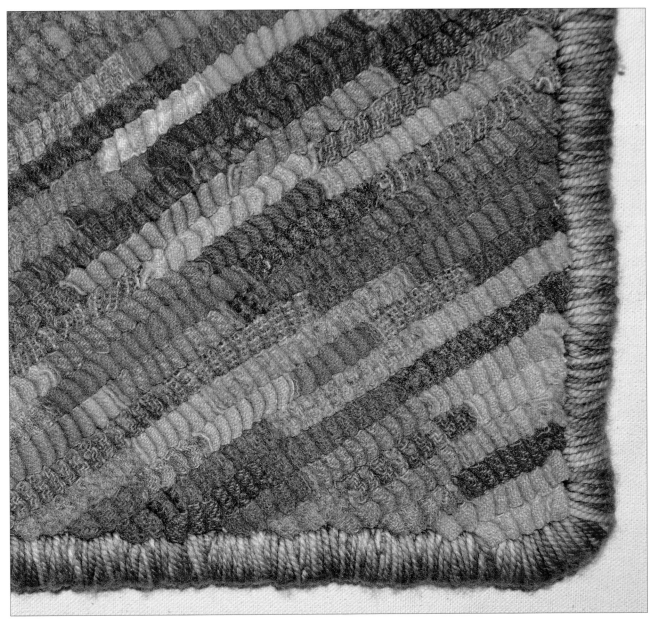

Diamond Trio, *detail with interval two-yarn whipping (see the full rug on page 62).*

but thought it would be too strong and dominant along the edge, so she combined a strand of the blue with the red and whipped them together. The blue offers the visual continuity while the red offers up a gentle and subdued striping along the edge, giving the viewer one more pattern to appreciate from the field of three simple diamonds.

I have to say that sometimes a simple finish with yarn or strips in one color would be the best choice for a rug design where an edge with more fuss may be its undoing. The processes discussed here are given as just a few of many options. The objective is to encourage you to exercise artistic integrity in the choices you make for your rugs all the way to the end. Understandably, because rug hooking is a slow process, it is not an easy undertaking when we have become enamored with our next project and seek to get on with it as quickly as possible. But the joys of persisting in aesthetic mode all the way to the end will deepen the satisfaction with the final results. Remember that the future projects will wait, and just a little bit of patience in the finishing of your current project will reward you ten-fold for years to come. After all, we who hook rugs have it in our nature to love the journey as much as the destination.

Chapter 6

The Creative Stitches

We have looked at color and how low contrast blending brings a note of interest to our rugs. We can look back to our early hooking careers when pulling up loops was a challenge in and of itself. Back then, our focus was on the mechanics of the art and we were quite accepting of the simplicity of the outline and fill method as well as the simple outcome of compositions that we were executing. As hooking became easier, we discovered that the hooking rhythms were a pleasure all their own. Then, there came the point where we felt ready to explore a few more challenges as we continued to learn in workshops and from our hooking friends.

If you want to add pizzazz to your work, creative stitches have the potential to create some real spark. Like other elements that go into creating balance in your work (like color and value), the creative stitches call for judicious assessment. They work best when incorporated in a balanced distribution throughout your design. If you confine them to one area of your rug, they will anchor the eye to that one spot to the detriment of the rest of your composition. They have a powerful capacity to engage the eye, and the balance of your composition must be strong enough to elicit sufficient atten-

tion in their presence. A light spark of creative stitches, however, can certainly be the final and perfect touch for what you are trying to accomplish.

It's best to use creative stitches sparingly at first. This will acquaint you to the vibrancy inherent in them. As your eye becomes more adept at harnessing their energy, your aesthetic sensibilities and comfort level will grow.

The strategies here are probably familiar; I hope that mentioning them will be a reminder and encouragement to use them in your upcoming projects.

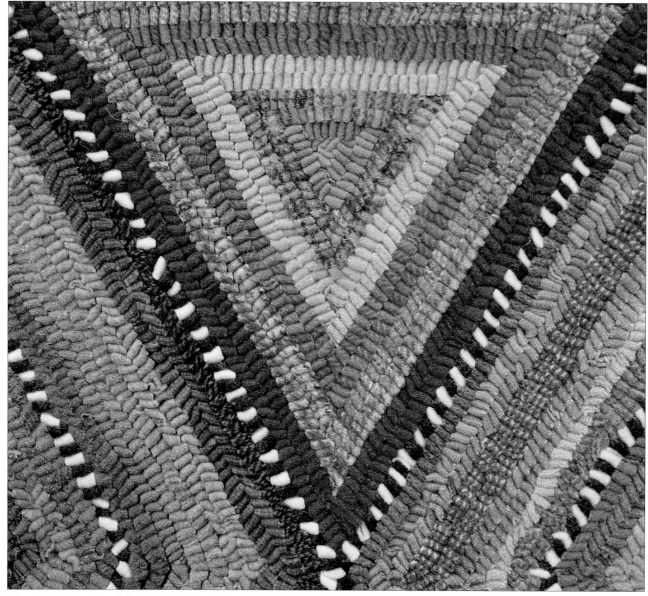

Diamond Trio, *detail showing black-and-white beaded stitch (see the full rug on page 68).*

BEADING

Most of us have seen beading and have even used it in our rugs. It is simple in its structure and easy enough for most beginners to pick up. It is also the basis for other stitches in this chapter. Beading is a good way to use up precut strips (that match in width) to embellish smaller motifs like flower petals or leaves. Try using beading along the inside edge of a border. Here are the steps to get you started:

1. Begin with two contrasting strips—one light, one dark—and pull both of their tails up through the top.

2. Insert a hook into the backing. With the hand below, feed only one of the strips (Strip A) onto the hook. Pull that strip to the top, forming a loop at the desired height.

3. Put a hook into the backing to form the next loop. This time, feed the alternate strip (Strip B) onto the hook and bring the loop up to the surface at the desired height.

4. Continue alternating Strips A and B to the ends of the strips. Bring the tails to the surface, and trim them to slightly beneath the loop height. If one strip runs out before the other, bring the new strip's tail into the same hole as the last loop formed and trim it beneath the loop height.

The Rugs Upon Which We Walk

You will notice a ridge on the back of the beaded stitch that is created by the switching back and forth of the two different strips. Like some things in the rug hooking world, controversy abounds about whether rugs with beading are suitable for use on the floor. The ridge on the back is said to be vulnerable to excessive stress underfoot and will wear out prematurely, needing repair before other areas of the rug. I don't think that it is within the scope of my experience to verify this or not, but I have seen many floor rugs holding up just fine.

The question remains then: how often will this ridge receive impact in relation to other parts of the rug? And if the beaded area is much more susceptible to wear, what kind of time frame are we considering? So, in theory, perhaps it does make sense to put these rugs in less trafficked areas, but I am of the opinion that these theories may have more a bearing in generational time spans as opposed to a single lifetime. I have seen rugs with beading that have been on the floor in people's homes for around 10 years and are no worse for the wear.

Enjoy your rugs as you display them in your homes for your pleasure.

MIX IT UP

Here's an idea you can try with the beading, checkerboard, or weaving stitch. There is no reason in the world why you have to use the same colors of wool throughout the entire space you are filling with these stitches. Since the objective is to use up your stash and whittle away at your strip bags, don't constrain yourself: feel free to use all the variations of one or both colors. Try different values of the two colors in the same area in your checkerboard and it will have a luminous glow. Using multiple values will attract the eye and compel the viewer to appreciate the variations in what would otherwise be a predictable pattern.

Spring Has Sprung, *detail showing checkerboard stitch (see the full rug on page 102).*

CHECKERBOARD STITCH

This fun stitch to make simply follows the beading technique, except that you do two loops of each color. The first row will go in easy. The second row will require a teensy bit more attention. After you have the first row in place, you will have established a vertical grid for subsequent rows.

The objective will be to line up each of the loops directly beneath the loops previously established in Row 1. If your first two loops

were light blue alternated with two loops of red, for instance, then you will do the opposite in Row 2. Begin with the red strip and make sure your loops are directly below the light blue loops. Continue with the same patterning across the row and keep each color directly beneath its oppositional color to the end. Row 3 will go back to the Row 1 sequence. Continue alternating row patterns working your way down the space.

Little Posie, *decorative stitch sampler.*

Creative stitches will add powerful interest to your rugs if you use them in a balanced way. Treat them like you would any color; distribute the techniques throughout your rug.

- *Vase–checkerboard stitch*
- *Leaves–cobblestone stitch*
- *Leaves outline–chain stitch*
- *Tulip–weaving stitch*
- *Tulip outline–beading stitch*

WEAVING STITCH

This stitch is a combination of beading and standard hooking. The one caveat is that you must be mindful of the grid that will be necessary for all of the loops to line up. Here is how to work the weaving stitch:

1. Work one row of beading with two alternating colors.
2. The second row is straight hooking with the choice of one of the colors in the beading row. Hook the loops directly below the loops of the beaded row.
3. Continue alternating a beaded row with a solid row, making sure to keep the rows directly in line (vertically) with all the loops.

Detail of weaving stitch with beaded outline.

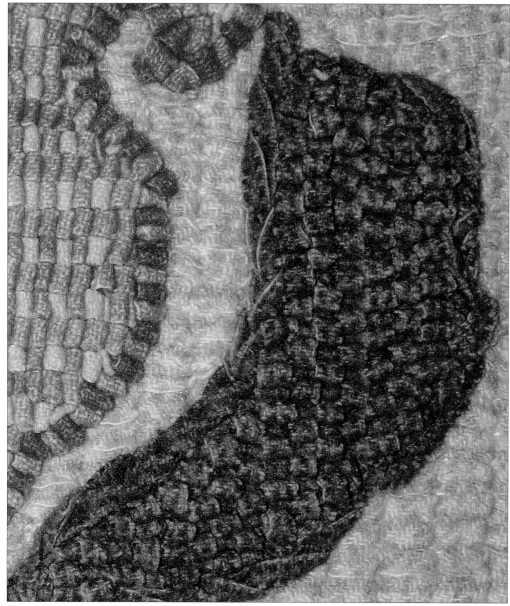

Little Posie, *detail showing cobblestone stitch.*

COBBLESTONE STITCH

This stitch really plays up the texture of rug hooking. It will bring an added dimension to any motif and can also be used to outline motifs or highlight the inside edge of borderlines. Here is how you do it:

Begin by pulling up your first loop to standard height. Pull the second loop at least 30% higher. Continue hooking, alternating the loop heights—one standard (low) height, one high—all across the first row.

On the second row, keep your loops directly beneath the Row 1 loops. Under the low loop, hook a high loop. The next loop, directly under the high loop in Row 1, will be a low loop. Continue alternating and creating a checkerboard pattern with all the loops lined up vertically.

Cobblestone stitch in gold. Chain stitch in aqua on top and bottom borders.

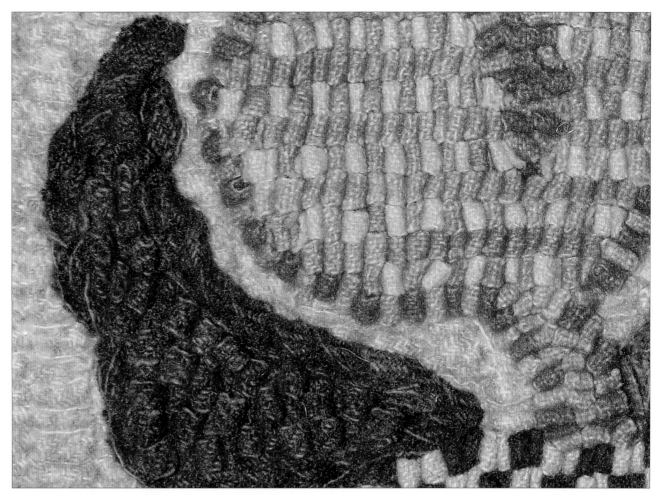

Little Posie, *detail showing chain stitch in outline of leaf.*

CHAIN STITCH

I have been enamored with chain stitch embroidery in textiles of the Middle East and Central Asia for a number of years now. I have it in my mind to create a rug just using the chain stitch because it works up much faster using the hook and strips of wool.

If you have any experience with crochet, this stitch should be second nature to you. It is much shallower than the loop height as it lies flatter against the backing and looks like a braid. Plan to use longer than usual strips as they get taken up much faster, too. Here are the steps:

1. Begin with a strip folded about 2" underneath the backing. Insert the hook into the linen from the top and pull up half the loop formed by the fold. Leave about $1/2$" of the tail end underneath.

2. Moving in an upward direction toward the left and keeping the hook in the loop, advance the hook to the next space about $1/2$" away. Grab a strip from under the backing, and pull up another loop; this time pull the strip up through the first loop until all that remains is the second loop on the hook. Repeat the chaining to the near end of the strip leaving 1" dangling under the backing.

3. To add another strip, leave the hook on the last loop. Fold the strip 2" as in the beginning, and pull a loop of the new strip up through the last loop of the previous strip, leaving both tails under the backing.

4. To end, form one last loop and pull the strip up to the top of the backing. Take the strip, overlap the last loop, and push it down to the underside into same hole that it came through.

5. Turn the rug to the back, and tuck the loose tail ends into the back of the chain stitching.

Gallery Walk

Scrappy rugs come in many variations, but they can often be broadly grouped into three categories: hit and miss rugs, parts and pieces rugs, and blended rugs. We'll also take a look at scrappy rugs that combine two or more of these techniques.

There is much to learn by seeing examples of these different scrappy rug techniques. My one hope in presenting all the strategies and techniques here is that you may become intrigued with one or two aspects that you can then incorporate into a future rug and move toward the goal of discovering your personal scrappy style. The beauty of discovering one's style is that components of aesthetics will often speak to us if we stand ready to listen.

Be encouraged; there are lots of ways to play. The delights in our tactile craft will be ours to enjoy for years to come. With some forethought and planning, the joy can only increase!

HIT AND MISS RUGS

No mistake about it, hit and miss rugs have been the go-to technique for using up your scraps. They have provided a resolution for every overflowing strip bag through the centuries. Whether you have gathered a varied collection of colors or a limited selection of recycled garments, you will be able to use this method to eat away at your backlog of extra wool.

The history of the hit and miss technique was born out of resourcefulness. The rug hooker in olden times used what she had. The attitude that drove this approach was more serendipitous than planned. The rug hooker would grab from her bag of strips almost blindly and use whatever made contact with her grip. There were varying degrees of mindfulness applied in the decision process, and the main object was to use as much as they had available and put the worn clothing to good use.

The debate still wages on about how much

Diamond Trio, *40" x 24", #9-cut wool on linen. Designed by Bea Brock and hooked by Teena Mills, Dallas, Texas, 2013.*

Diamond Trio is essentially a two-color approach to a hit and miss rug. Teena went through her stash and culled everything from two complementary color families: reds/rusts and blues/greens. Her warm/cool palette is not altogether uncommon, but Teena stretched herself by using a wide spectrum of colors and values within each group. Upon close inspection you will see light olive greens, turquoises, and peacock blues. The red diamonds may read like they are red, but Teena alternated the reds with golds throughout. The blues and greens are also alternating rows, yet the entire design holds its blue and red appearance. This is surely not a blended look, but the mixed bunches of both color variations give movement to what would otherwise be a very static design.

The method of using slightly different colored strips of one family of colors in one space works particularly well when filling in large areas of color. You can then create definition between motifs or spaces by exaggerating contrast. This composition would also work well with light and dark approaches in lieu of the complements. Perhaps, if you look through your wool stash, you will find that you have a predominance of at least two color families that just happen to be complements. Or, if you have two groupings— say blues—from one color family, how about a play on lights and darks to create contrast?

decision making goes into a true hit and miss technique, but whether you want to be completely serendipitous or seriously decisive, the larger the spectrum of colors and values, the better.

Geometric designs were frequently used with hit and miss techniques as they limited the challenges to playing light against dark. As contemporary rug hookers, however, our palettes are infinitely broader due to the offerings of hand-dyed wool peddlers that abound at hooking events across the country and online. The approach now is still to use what we have available to us, but because of larger availability, we are able to be a little more studious in the course of color planning and constructing our rugs.

On the following pages are some fine examples of rugs hooked by today's rug hookers who seek to honor the hit and miss tradition yet hold true to their own personal aesthetics.

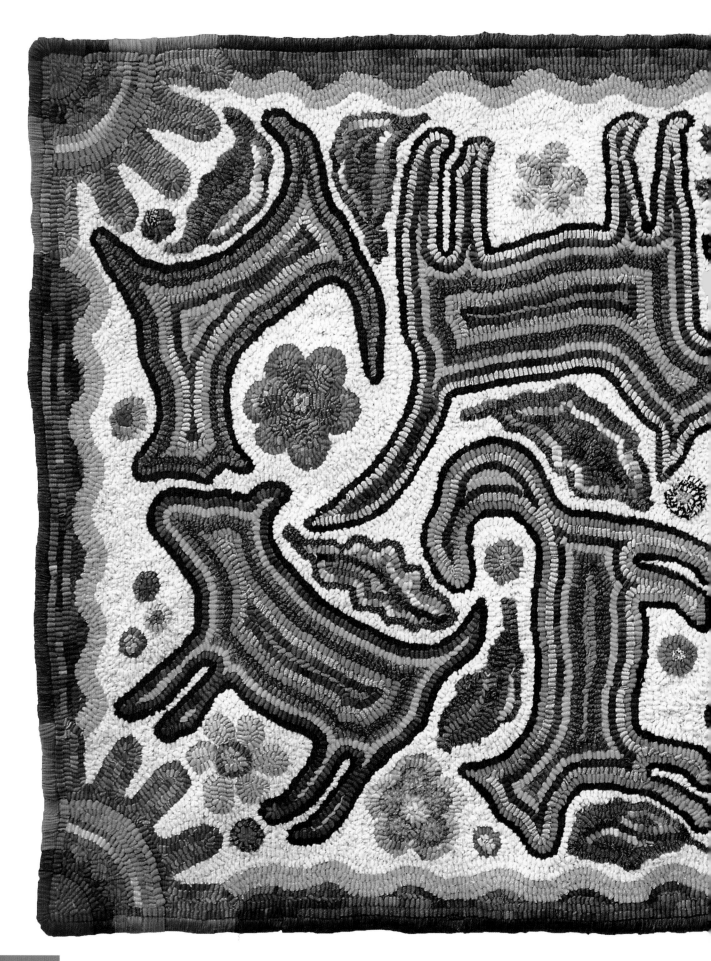

Patterned Pups, *40" x 29", #7-cut wool on linen. Designed by Bea Brock and hooked by Linda Huntley Wills, Rockwall, Texas, 2013.*

Still keeping within the hit and miss technique, Linda Wills took a different approach. Her wool collection contained a lot of scraps. Some were hand dyed, some were "as is" (new and recycled). With a lot of tidbits left over from previous projects, she was excited to work in a method that would help clean house a little.

Linda chose a pattern entitled Patterned Pups *but opted to ignore the interior design elements of the original "pups" and work with the silhouettes of the pups instead. Working concentrically within the silhouettes, she created an end result that is reminiscent of Mola cloths or reverse appliqué worked by the Kuna cultures of Central America. The success of this rug relies on good color distribution to bring balance to an otherwise very busy schematic.*

Scrappy Hooked Rugs

Gumball Track, *40" x 25½", #5- to 8-cut wool on linen. Designed by Bea Brock and hooked by Gina Paschall, Dallas, Texas, 2013.*

When we first think of the hit and miss technique, we usually associate it with straight line hooking as in the border of Gina Paschall's rendition of Gumball Track. But Gina took the hit and miss technique a step further by randomly breaking up the circles with concentric hit and miss hooking.

Keeping each circle similarly colored, but still using odd bits and pieces, she utilized beading every now and then to break from the regular bull's-eye treatment to add an unpredictable element to the overall composition. This could have easily gone the way of simple outline and fill, but the techniques used here make it an active and energetic composition. Using many light-colored woolens in the border effectively creates a frontal plane giving depth to the work, as well. With the myriad of colors represented here, this rug provides a good opportunity to emphasize the benefit of working with an organized stash.

Diamond Trio, 40" x 24", #8.5-cut wool on linen. Designed by
Bea Brock and hooked by Barbara Riley, Brazoria, Texas, 2013.

There is always some uncertainty when facing a new
pattern, especially in the scope of having a considerable
stash that is begging to become a part of the process. A
simple survey of Barbara Riley's ample stash made it clear
that this was going to be a work of complementary colors,
and Barbara's ever-growing stash lent itself to creating
intricacies within each color family.

Though this is not a hit and miss rug in the strictest
sense, Barbara's version of Diamond Trio has the feel of it
because of the abundant colors used. I could appropriately
label it as an expanded version of hit and miss because the
colors are used in family groupings to create the bands that
run along the diagonals of the diamonds and triangles.
Obviously a warm/cool approach to color, like Teena Mills's
Diamond Trio, this rug separates itself by enclosing the
triangles along the border, which brings those negative

spaces into almost equal prominence with the diamonds. Note that the outside diamonds match while the middle diamond gains a trifle more attention by its use of that one chartreuse stripe that reverberates against the light purple.

The beaded outlining is a wonderful visual surprise. It highlights the overall composition, and the choice of black and white provides a stark contrast against the predominately middle-valued woolens. This rug is evidence that one single decision, like the beaded outline,

can make all the difference in the world.

These rugs are by no means definitive of the hit and miss genre, but they do take the tradition into another realm when organization and planning are put to use, especially with all the wool colors available in today's market. With the palettes in each of the rugs being quite varied, each hooker made a studious assessment of her stash with selectivity while still preserving a visible evidence of randomness.

PARTS AND PIECES RUGS

Perhaps you don't have overflowing bags of precut strips but instead have parts and pieces of uncut wool in varying sizes left over from previous projects. Putting those oddments into one rug can be quite a challenge.

The first order of business is selecting or designing a pattern that requires an assortment of varied colors. Those colors can work together harmoniously, or they can represent a wide spectrum on the color wheel. If a pattern has a great number of small areas that can be taken up with many single small pieces, it should prove a great depository for your varied collection.

Posies in a Row, *40" x 30", #8- and #8 ¹/₂-cut wool on linen. Designed by Bea Brock and hooked by Karen Lea, Richmond, Texas, 2013.*

When working with a varied palette, it is important to have a background that will ground everything. Rug hookers know that going very dark or light will leave more options in choosing colors for motifs. In Posies in a Row, *Karen Lea selected a dark brown of differing woolens to support the colorful cast. The browns, though slightly different, are varied enough to create close-up interest but blended enough to hold together from a distance. With all of the colors in the rug, it is just one more pleasant surprise for the viewer.*

Notice the main center and corner daisy motifs. They are mixed values of the same raspberry color, but all the other motifs are filled in with single pieces of solidly dyed wool. Consider how using repetition in those daisy motifs brings a stabilizing factor in the field of the diverse colors. The use of the off-white colors throughout adds a strong contrast as well as continuity and a grounding repetition to the composition.

The success of Karen's rug comes with a stylistic mildly muted palette. If you collect wool colors you love and find yourself reaching for the same hues, remember to enhance your collection with differing values of your favorites. The variety in values or subtle differences in tone will contribute highlights and cohesiveness to your design. Take a closer look at Karen's piece and notice the subtle differences in the pinks she used. There you will find a healthy spectrum of lighter cotton candy pinks and light corals going all the way to the rich raspberry pinks in the daisies. A veritable candy store of color!

A well-designed parts and pieces pattern is welcoming to all kinds of palettes, be it a muted one like Karen's, or jewel toned, or bright and contemporary. Infusing your palette with variety in hue and tone will energize the design.

With this type of scrappy rug, you will more than likely find yourself hooking speedily as there is little requirement for stopping and changing color within a given area. It makes for great hooking fun in the process.

IN SEARCH OF A COLOR PLAN

You have your pattern in hand, and are staring hard at it while waiting for the perfect color plan to come to mind that will carry you to the fabulous finish. Nothing comes. Now what?

You can avoid these crises once and for all by keeping track of your evolving tastes in a notebook. Have you ever flipped through a magazine and were stopped dead in your tracks by a luscious photograph of a textile, a quilt, a garment, or wallpaper? As you forage through your wardrobe, is there a printed fabric on a certain garment that you just love to wrap around yourself? These are things that you absolutely love, so why not keep a record of them in a special place where you can go back to them time and time again for inspiration?

Take that blouse with the fabulous print and photograph it, or even better, lay it on the glass of your printer and make a colored print of it. Have your notebook filled with empty page protectors where magazine pages and color prints will be stored for posterity. Tear out that magazine page and file it in one of those page protectors. Before you know it, you will have a notebook filled with examples of color plans that will be an inspiring resource to cull from when you are in need.

Write notes on each one and drop that in the sleeve too. Ask yourself questions about why it has been placed among the honored ideas in your notebook. What are the dominant and subordinate colors? How important is the background color? Answering these questions will help you decide how to distribute those very colors in your next rug.

Gypsy Wagon, *38¹/₂" x 26¹/₂", #6- to 8.5-cut wool on linen. Designed by Bea Brock and hooked by Melody Lundquist, Irving, Texas, 2013.*

Gypsy Wagon *was also designed for an open and diverse palette. In this rendering, Melody Lundquist brings a vintage look by way of the muted gold background. Her wool stash contained some jewel tones and muted wool, and her approach to color placement looks like it was dependent on the number of repeats throughout. Sometimes if the repetition in your design adds up to a good number, you can plan your color distribution according to the repetition.*

In the border are a total of 28 circular motifs, including the corner ones. Melody was wise to go with that repetition, and her four main colors are equally distributed all around the edge seven times and represented twice in the daisies. How lucky can a hooker get with just a little bit of thinking and counting?

Moving to another color altogether—red—gave the composition some stability in much the same way that Karen Lea's daisy motifs did in Posies in a Row. *This change worked, not only because red is a commanding color, but also because it was used in repetition in very central locations. It is natural for the eye to first explore the center of any given format and from there dance across the space to further explore the activity around the edges. And with the daisies and the border "sticks" and dots executed in the same background color of the red crosses, the stability is all the more enhanced.*

Gridded Crosses, *39" x 13½", #6-cut wool on linen. Designed by Bea Brock and hooked by Jaci Clements, Dallas, Texas, 2013.*

On the surface, this design is simply a rendering of two differently sized squares. Not too difficult to create, but Jaci Clements's execution, albeit simple straight-across hooking, takes on a style reminiscent of the Arts and Crafts movement. Upon initial impact, the viewer is transported to a Frank Lloyd Wright house and the simple stained glass windows that adorned homes in that period.

Though no discernible pattern is used in the color distribution, balance is achieved by the predominance of middle value tones against the cream background. The darker crosses are disbursed apart from each other and contribute just enough depth to create interest. Using parts and pieces of leftover wool from previous projects, Jaci included different values that give it a luminescent glow. Upon close inspection, the larger squares seem to come from about three different cream-colored or off-white pieces. The shifting light in these woolens is just one more feature that adds to the delight.

KNOW THYSELF

I have often asked the question, "How do we make decisions about what pattern to design or purchase?" A loaded question indeed, but identifying those clues that abide in each and every one of us can lead to the possibility of discovering a style, which is a worthy goal for anyone engaged in artistic endeavors.

What appeals to us is strongly connected to our identity. In the artistic life, making that strong connection to who we are and what we create is an ongoing process. Look around your homes, your closets, your books and magazines. Is there a preponderance of colors repeated there? Is there evidence of rigid lines, undulating lines, or geometry in the prints that you clothe yourself with?

Discovering these things first and acknowledging them thereafter will bring decisiveness in the choices you make for your art. Being authentic to those design elements that pervade your environment will strongly connect you to the choices you make in the rugs you hook or any other artistic occupation that fills your days.

"Know thyself." It is the channel that will bring about honest artistic expression in your work.

Color Pies, *40" x 30", #5- to 8-cut wool on linen. Designed and hooked by Bea Brock, Kerrville, Texas, 2012.*

Color Pies is another pattern that was designed for the parts and pieces floating around that you might like to clear out. Each wedge in the color pie (with minor exceptions) can be filled with one piece of wool.

In this version, I occasionally repeated that one wool color in another wedge in the composition— if it was large enough, as there were many wedges that needed to be filled. The outcome of this work is largely based on creating contrast in the scope of all the colors used. The outlines of the wedges were randomly chosen to carefully avoid duplication nearby. All the colors in the wedges were selected for maximum contrast with their neighboring wedges, both within the color pie and in adjacent color pies as well. Coupling all this against a seriously dark chocolate background places the attention securely upon the dancing color throughout the rug.

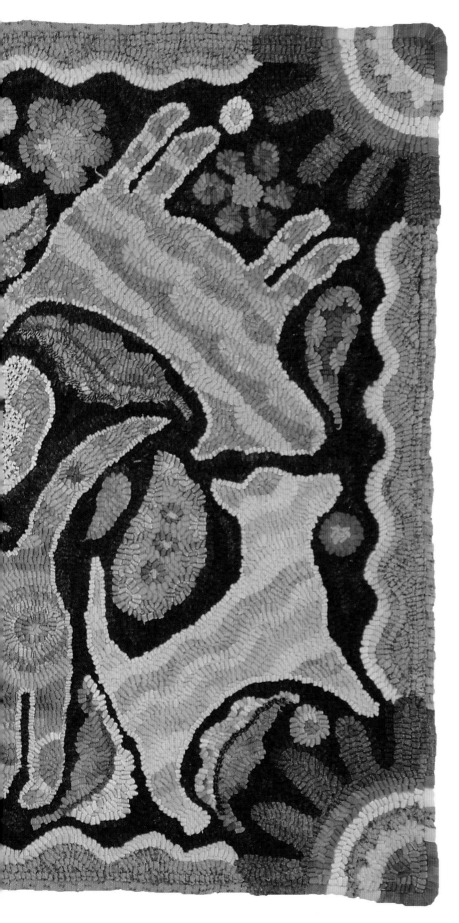

Patterned Pups, *40" x 29", #4- and 8-cut, wool on linen. Designed by Bea Brock and hooked by Honey Gill, Tyler, Texas, 2013.*

Who among us does not like puppies? If the silhouettes were not enough to evoke the captivating charm of a litter of puppies, Honey Gill takes it up a notch with whimsical carnival-like colors. Whimsy is like that—it pulls us into a world away from everyday concerns.

Honey kept each of the puppies within one color family. In each puppy, there is a small spectrum of contrast within the patterning that keeps the silhouette more solid. If you look closely, you will see that she also outlined each one with the lightest of tints; that helps the shape stay intact against the very dark brown background.

The border is subordinated to the main design. Honey uses all the colors in the pups in the corner motifs in a more subdued tone. This keeps the coloring connected to the overall composition without dominating it.

Observe how Honey used the minor motifs in the color play. You will notice that each of the main colors in the pups is distributed in other parts of the design. For example, check out the yellow pup in the lower right hand corner and search for where yellow or gold is used elsewhere. You will find it in the small circle at the top left, in between the tails of the purple and blue pups in the leaf, in the small circle under the green pup's nose, on top of the green pup's back in the leaf, and in the leaf between the pink and purple pups. The yellow is not repeated on the third of the area where the yellow pup is, but it is sprinkled in the remainder of the field. This promotes balance in the composition.

Noticing how others distribute color in their rugs is a good learning exercise. It is good to slow down enough to appreciate the decisions that others make to create balance. When you use a color in one area, be sure to disburse it in some form (be it a light, dark, or tonal version) across your design.

Rebecca Jr., *36" x 36", #6- to 8-cut wool on linen. Designed by Bea Brock and hooked by Mary Ruelle, Fredericksburg, Texas, 2009.*

Mary Ruelle used a medium blended effect in her hooking of Rebecca Jr. The varied values used are definitely more apparent in some areas than others. If you look at the gold background behind the daisy center, you can appreciate the presence of a wider spectrum of values of gold. The placement does create a striated movement, but not so much that the readability of the repeat is disrupted. The rust-colored scallops around the ring are more closely matched but disparate enough to give the rug an added textural read.

RIGHT: Carly, *33" x 22", #7-cut wool on linen. Designed by Bea Brock and hooked by Brenda McGee, Lorena, Texas, 2013.*

This simple little design was less than impressive in a black-and-white drawing. It was designed with circle templates and very little else, other than the center flower. As with many simple patterns, it is a challenge to know where to begin to bring life to the design. Brenda McGee, however, instantly saw potential for a grandchild's nursery. Brenda had some sizeable wool pieces in her stash. She is an accomplished dyer, so she pulled six colors (including the outline) from her ample hand-dyed collection that would be perfect. There was no complex planning for this rug as she knew she had enough to make it all the way around with each color row. Her outline provides the glue that pulls it all together and adds a subdued cast to keep the colors from getting too sugary.

Two rows of bronze around the outer perimeter narrow the outer border a tad, but they set up for a perfectly coordinated binding that brings it all to a great finish. The final punch to the design is the depth of dark reds in the center, and the playful outlined circles incorporate all the colors used in the rug. Brenda's choices incorporating both the simple and the playful resulted in a rug that was perfectly suited for its intended purpose.

Ring Toss, *33" x 28½", #6- to 8-cut wool on linen. Designed by Bea Brock and hooked by Paty Parish Pitts, Dallas, Texas, 2013.*

Ring Toss has a lot in common with Square in a Square and Patterned Pups. They are all open vessels for color. You don't have to worry about representing something in nature or a still life. All these patterns call for are for you to dig deep into your love of color and get in every variety of wool that is in your stash. If you remember to watch for contrast with every choice, you will succeed in adding "pop" to your rug.

The pattern design is a simple outlay of rectangles and circles and was easily designed using a compass, ruler, and a set of circle templates. Paty Parish Pitts's wool stash is vibrant and offered her plenty of choices for a wide spectrum of color, all comparably intense. She created clarity in the rings of single rows by using complements or a switch-up in the value. With this veritable "jelly bean jar" color plan, Paty used a very dark outline in all the straight edges to contain the boxes of colors. Looking at all of the bull's-eye circles, you can see how all the strips and small pieces in her stash finally made it into a rug.

Note, too, the alternating aqua and light olive bands that back up the circles. Because they are lighter than the motifs, they create a soft backdrop of alternating color. The bands offer rest in the field of undulating color.

TO SHADE OR NOT TO SHADE

A discussion of rug hooking history would not be complete without addressing the era of what is known as "fine shading." In my earlier hooking days, it did not take long for me to recognize that there were two distinct camps in the rug hooking world. You were either of the "fine shading" persuasion or the "primitive" persuasion. I've seen the last 20 years soften the boundaries of these two distinctions, and rugs that defy the distinction show up frequently in rug shows.

I am particularly enamored with rugs that incorporate "mock shading," using the variations of textures, values, and tones to subtly express a suggestive dimensional quality that does not dominate the rug. Once the apex of hooking achievement, shading has now been relegated to one tool among many others to be used in personal expression. I have used a plethora of textures, solids, plaids, or anything that will mimic gradation without being too fussy about imitating perfectly graded swatches. This casual approach brings a folksy character to rugs, while taking the hooker away from the stress of technical perfection. It makes shading still fun to do.

Choosing to use shading, whether the "mock" or "fine" variety, is your choice. How much shading do you like in your rugs? What do you feel when looking at finely shaded rugs? Is shading the main objective in a rug? Or is there a greater message to be communicated apart from technical execution? If you are attracted to more subtle executions of shading, are you compelled to imitate that in your work? An honest response to those questions will help you decide what kind of shading is compatible with your personal style.

Scrappy Hooked Rugs

Square in a Square,
40½" x 27", #8.5-cut wool on linen. Designed by Bea Brock and hooked by Ginger Smith, Midlothian, Texas, 2013.

Like Ring Toss, Square in a Square *utilizes the same outlining and provides a slight measure of more definition between the color bands of the squares. That dark brown delineation also leads the eye to the border background and serves to keep the eye moving throughout. Ginger, an avid dyer, stepped out of her comfort zone with the vibrant selection of colors used here.*

An interesting thing that happens with simple geometrics that have comparably equally sized motifs is that the color play takes on a more planar dynamic. Colors pop forward toward the viewer while some recede, and still others stay in the middle ground. Some hot spots might be created where a turquoise will vibrate against an orange or an orange against chartreuse. It is a daring thing to create this vibrancy, but the reward is always eye opening and energetic.

Dresden in the Vine, *18" x 18", #6-cut wool.*
Designed by Bea Brock and hooked by Judy Bruns,
Brenham, Texas, 2013.

Judy Bruns put a small collection of reds,
greens, and golds to use in Dresden in the Vine.
When you have a specific number of repeated
parts, you can come up with a numerical repeat
that will fit just right. There are 12 wedges here,
and Judy's repeat of four colors makes perfect
sense. The different golds holding up in their lighter
value are the perfect colors to sit against the red
background. The final finish of the border incorpo-
rating all of the colors in the design was perfectly
separated by the light gold row traveling around
the parameter of the design. This pattern may be
small, but the completed rug is filled with big ideas!

YOUR PERSONAL COLOR STYLE

These scrappy rugs are only a handful of suggestions in the
ocean of possibilities; the bottom line to choose colors and
color combinations that move and inspire you. These days we all
live busy lives, but even in the flurry of everyday life, we are
sometimes pierced by overwhelming beauty that takes us to another plane. Beauty in color is to be found everywhere by just
slowing down and moving through our world with open eyes.
Perhaps a window arrangement at your local mall pulls your eye
in or a fabric print you see on someone walking past you makes
you look twice. Remembering those visual experiences are
clues to what is unique in you, and they can be the stepping-
stones that lead you to your own personal color style.

Lacy Heart, *36" x 36", #6- to 8-cut wool on linen. Designed by Bea Brock and hooked by Alison Auckland, New Ulm, Texas, 2013.*

Alison Auckland's selection of the Lacy Heart *pattern was initially filled with uncertainty. After all, an initial inspection of the line work looked tedious and overwhelming. Once Alison decided upon a strategy and began working, peace prevailed.*

Alison's wool stash showed her propensity for buying certain colors over and over again because of her love for them. Her mild obsession turned out to be very handy in that a lot of the wools were close in value and worked very well together. Anywhere from three to five different woolens are represented for every colored section. The blending is visibly smoother or flatter in some areas, but this variation adds to the overall charm of the finished rug and keeps the viewer's eye engaged in the unpredictability of tone throughout.

A technique of note is the use of olive brown outlining throughout the composition as room allowed. This olive brown brings the overall color plan a more muted cast that is perfectly in line with how Alison likes her rugs.

THE BLENDED RUGS

A few years ago, I was in the middle of a rug project and was having conniptions over the challenges it was presenting me. I was anticipating attending a hook-in about three hours from home and was hoping that decisions would surface before leaving, so that once I got there, I could continue hooking this rug without having to make crucial decisions in the midst of all the social distractions that make hook-ins so fun. Well, the aesthetic resolutions were not forthcoming, and I was in a mild panic. The evening before leaving, I did make one fortuitous decision: I decided to abandon the current project and take (what I call) a "no brainer" pattern with me.

Once that decision was made, I felt like a free woman. I went to my studio closet, found a large scrap of linen, cut it down the middle, and reshaped it to a long runner. I was in the mood for a serious runner. I marked the ends for a 3" overlap, serged both pieces, and basted them together. My runner measured 30" x 8'. I marked the perimeters by running a marker down the

grain, added a 1" border, and very loosely drew diagonal lines that would eventually become my *Wonky Diamonds* pattern.

With my previous rug still weighing on me, I was determined to set myself up with pure color play. I filled up my ample canvas bag with every piece of scrap available and forced in a few bags of leftover strips. I was armed and ready, anticipating a run of days for just pure color fun. Therein was the joy of this blended scrappy rug.

THE JOY OF COLOR

Working on *Wonky Diamonds* led me to the pure joys that are inherent in just playing with color, leaving other considerations like balance, realism, depth or color planning completely out of the process. My decisions were reduced to "What color will show up best next to the last color used?" and "Is the next color choice a good distance away from where it was last used?" These two questions are, in a nutshell, how I strategize color balance. I love the clarity of shape that is accomplished by making sure that colors used in proximity to each other will define the edge that separates adjoining spaces. That became clear in the process of hooking *Wonky Diamonds*.

I mention this because working purely with color allows all other formal aesthetic concerns to go by the wayside, leaving the rug hooker the isolated experience of juxtaposing colors with each other. In the process, we learn not just what colors we love, but what colors we love to combine with each other. Perhaps this is an exercise that will open your eyes and mind to simple color issues that originate with inexperience or indecision. Choosing or designing a simple geometric pattern that will open the observing mind to the interrelationship of color is a good way to explore what is inside you, as exploration and discovery invariably accompany one another.

Wonky Diamonds, *96" x 30", #5- to 8.5-cut wool on linen. Designed and hooked by Bea Brock, Kerrville, Texas, 2011.*

My ongoing objective in hooking Wonky Diamonds *was to use up as much of my precut strips and small pieces as possible. Since I had the wool scraps in separate bags organized by color, I worked one bag at a time, pulling strips that were somewhat close in value, and hooked concentrically around the diamond edge from the outside in.*

Because each bag was a conglomeration of variations of one color, I chose the strips by selecting one that was a slight shift in value from the one used previously. For the diamonds themselves, choosing what colors went next to each other was a simple matter of picking a color that would be a contrast to the diamond next door. I worked on the short end with the diamonds going across and made my way (8') to the other end, being mindful to not place the same color (or color grouping) too close to itself or a similar color.

Working with the color focus was so invigorating that I finished the hooking in a matter of eight weeks. The added bonus of consuming a substantial stash of strips made the experience even better!

Wonky Diamonds, *52" x 30", #6- to 8-cut wool on linen. Designed by Bea Brock and hooked by Martha Reynolds, Dallas, Texas.*

Martha Reynolds had held a longstanding ambition to hook a red rug, her favorite color. For the Wonky Diamonds *red version, Martha pulled out anything*

remotely red in her stash (there was a lot!) and sorted it into groups that would blend with each other. There were groups of tomato reds, wine reds, fire engine reds, orangey reds, pinkish reds; every variation of red that exists had made a home in Martha's wool room for quite some time, and now was the time to come to reckoning with her ambition as well

as her overstuffed shelves. Along with all the reds, she chose variations of gold for the dividing lines and border.

Initially, her first attempts were to create a sequencing pattern, but she came to the resolve that she would just have to work it out as she went along. The final outcome owes its success to the mix of each grouping. The fluctua-tions in value give it the textural look of an intuitive pastel painting. The richness of the red and gold woolens also makes for a very medieval castle-like appointment. The success of the rug is owed to the random look of color place-ment, and the viewer is thereby treated to a celebration of Martha's favorite color.

Scrappy Hooked Rugs

Calliope, *38" x 26", #5- to 7-cut wool on linen. Designed by Bea Brock and hooked by Janet Griffith, Plano, Texas, 2013.*

Janet Griffith's Calliope *has a very soft, blended look, like a blended pastel painting, that is accentuated by the dark brown line work. The design is predominantly like a pen and ink drawing, giving it a very lacy feel. At first impact from a distance, the viewer might think only six colors were used. But the hidden surprise comes with a closer inspection when you realize that within each field of color are uncountable variations. This hidden find compels the viewer to appreciate the unexpected complexity in all of the combinations used.*

Talavera I, *41" x 28", #5- to 8-cut wool on linen. Designed by Bea Brock and hooked by Carol Rippa, San Antonio, Texas, 2013.*

The colors in Talavera I rep-resent a true complementary color plan. Upon closer inspec-tion, each of the colored areas is riddled with various tones that give each of its parts distinctive color reads. The big Xs are con-trasted by their values, which give the rug the major popping rhythm, but the subtle surprises are in the daisies that are part of the minor rhythm. They are close in value, but their color shifts create an alternating rhythm that is in keeping with the design. Take note of the common outline strategy used here and its contribution to the overall cohesiveness of the rug.

Topsy Turvy Chickens, *36" x 22", #6- to 8.5-cut wool on linen. Designed and hooked by Bea Brock, Kerrville, Texas, 2006.*
    The interesting thing about playing with a broad spectrum of values is that you can apply more or less texture just by virtue of using different values within one space. In the Topsy Turvy Chickens *there is an evident movement that is created by resorting to that wider spectrum. Because the shapes are simple, and the contrast*

between the motifs and the background is strong, the clarity of the design is not lost. Note too, that this strong contrast eliminated the necessity of outlining. This rug is an example of using a wider value base yet still working within a single color family. An ongoing question to experiment with is "How wide a value spectrum can be used without losing clarity of motifs?"

Big Star, *36" x 24", #8.5-cut wool on linen. Designed and hooked by Bea Brock, Kerrville, Texas, 2013.*

Big Star *is a play on variations of contrast. The center* star, being the most luminous, is flanked by squares of warmth to boost an already glowing aquamarine. The final creation of depth is established by the dark striping of the

background. All areas of color are combinations of wool with the exception of the common outline in a bronze-colored brown. Those combinations, because they have *visible variances in value, add a serendipitous glimmer throughout and add interest to an otherwise rigidly designed pattern.*

COMBINED TECHNIQUES

Some of the rugs shown in this gallery were predominantly executed in one technique, either hit and miss done with a lot of leftover strips; parts and pieces done with small sections of wool and used independently in small spaces; or the blended method using many close values to fill elements. In the interest of opening up our options, it is important to appreciate that combining the techniques will make for very interesting rugs, though it will require a modicum af astuteness to use varying techniques in a balanced way. In this section, you'll find some examples of how a combination of techniques were used in any number of ways.

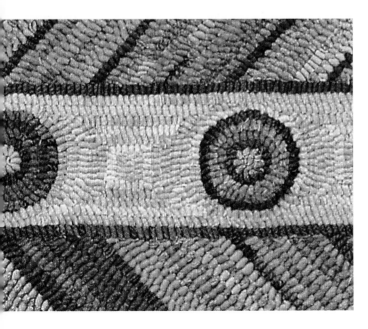

Mission Door, *48" x 18", #6- and 8-cut wool on linen. Designed by Bea Brock and hooked by Janie Staples, Arlington, Texas, 2013.*

If you want to crank out a rug in no time, give straight line hooking a try! You will be amazed at how fast you can fill up that linen. Janie Staples hooks fast to begin with, so it was no surprise that this rug zipped in and out of her hands in a matter of a few weeks. The woolens used here represent every color in the rainbow, and within each of the bars are subtly blended shades that give the rug a painterly overall appearance. To pull all the colors together, Janie used a cinnamon brown outline throughout.

The lighter valued gold cross pops up above the jewel-toned bars to give it an added planar dimension. Without the solidly filled cross, the overall textural quality would have been a little too repetitive and bland. What a difference it makes to be set off by the clarity of the cross and the solidly filled circles within it. The trick is to play with repetition but bring in something to add a little spark to diminish the predictability of the predictable.

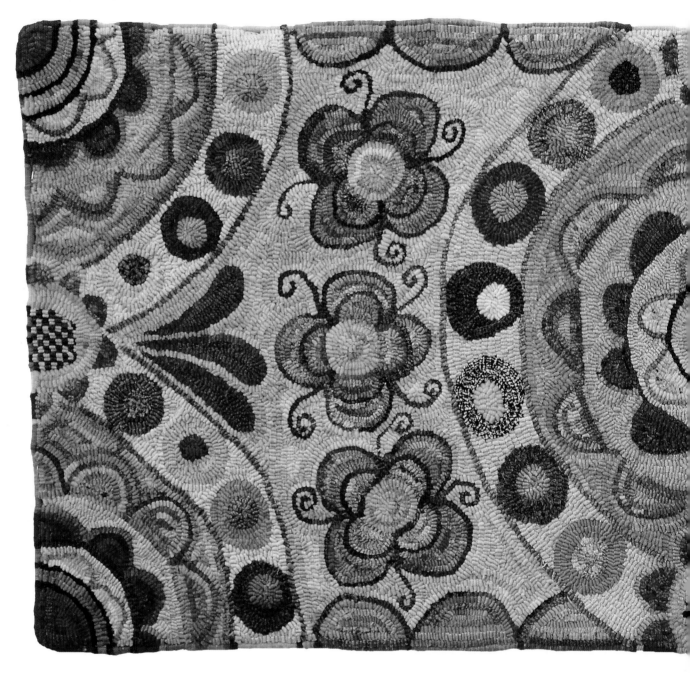

Spring Has Sprung, *52" x 24", wool on linen. Designed and hooked by Bea Brock, Kerrville, Texas, 2008.*

The design and execution of this pattern has served as the basis for many lessons over the years. It originated from a three-minute doodle in my sketchbook. The design is undoubtedly symmetrical overall, but the color placement is unpredictable. Predictability often renders a symmetrical, repeat pattern design static.

Look at the large central motif. Note that complements and value shifts help the amorphous scallops around the rings remain clear against the background. The scallops are a blend of strips and pieces in many tones and values of color, while the backgrounds are worked in a closer range of tones, resulting in a flat appearance. The "fried eggs" in the blue field bands are random, using up many 1" - 2" strips

that had been lying around for years. The one critical rule that I followed is that the circles had to be stark enough in color to stand out against the blue bands without being too repetitious.

The center edge floral motifs bring a crispness to the edge with their checkerboard stitches in turquoise and purple. Using the creative stitches can be a bit risky in such small spaces, but because the design and coloring are so active, the center edges gladly share the spotlight in a subdued way.

This rug was executed entirely from the scrap pile, with the exception of the cabbage green background behind the large red and purple background. The greens throughout partner up with the cool blues to bring cohesion to what could have been a fractured design.

Funky Southwest, *39" x 23", #6-cut wool on linen. Designed by Bea Brock and hooked by Ann Deane, Murchison, Texas, 2013.*

Ann Deane's Funky Southwest *has an appeal similar to that of* Mission Door *by way of their jewel-toned color*

plans. Here in Ann's rug, however, the reds are more dominant. The reds that encircle the larger round motifs in the center have a slightly visible disparity in their values, which adds a wonderful radiating directional quality to the middle background. Ann also cleverly works beading into

the larger and smaller circles, giving them all a textural edge that is still remarkable against the scrubbed shades that back them up. This balance is achieved by ensuring some serious contrast in the two colors of strips (blackish brown and light olive) that are used for the beaded edge so that they are clearly seen against the medium dark reds. The solid turquoise rings against the textures and reds give it an added pop. Her exceedingly dark brown (almost black) outline throughout brings cohesiveness to this multicolored funky design.

Jessica's Garden, *51" x 30", #6- to 8-cut wool on linen.*
Designed by Bea Brock and hooked by Janie Staples,
Arlington, Texas, 2008.

Jessica's Garden *is a step away from the geometric and*
into the realm of free flowing and undulating motifs; the
pattern typifies the combined techniques style. Upon first
glance at the drawing on the linen, the many different parts
can seem overwhelming, but addressing the challenge will
certainly make use of a varied scrap collection as the some-

what symmetrical design assists in achieving balance. All
of the motifs, with the exception of the sprawling center fern
and the top right and left corner sprigs, were hooked using
single pieces of wool in symmetrical fashion. And here, once
again, is the common use of a very dark plum-colored
background, which serves as the foil to all of the lustrous
color.

The simple key to the color use in Jessica's Garden *is*
the pursuit of contrast. All colors used in proximity to each

other are used for maximum contrast. There are no subtleties here. The rule is to make each section show up
at its maximum thereby creating an even playing field for
each motif calling for attention. It is almost an "all or
nothing" proposition. Each motif must be stark in its own
right to have a place of visibility in the overall composition.
The movement of the eye is then entrusted to the directional
quality of the design to keep the viewer engaged.

All parts of the rug were straightforward outline and fill

with one fabric assigned to the space. Of exception are the
two sprigs at the top right- and left-hand corners and the
bottom fern that sprawls out angularly from the center
bottom. There you will see a blended effect used amidst
all the flat outline and fill motifs. Despite the difference in
techniques used to hook these exceptions, they remain
an integral part of the composition due to clever use of
contrast.

Abigail, *39" x 30", #6- to 8-cut wool, designed by Bea Brock, hooked by Mary Ruelle, Fredericksburg, Texas, 2013.*

The design of Abigail *was influenced by paper-cutting techniques. The initial impression upon the viewer is that the rug is created by the use of single wool pieces that fill the wedges. The center Dresden plates repeat the colors in varying values, and the extra use of red in the "commas" brings the eye to the center focal point.*

The dual appeal of this rug is that the corner motifs, however, are executed using a blend of different woolens in close value and tone. Mary's rendition gives the rug a very lacy effect despite the large size of the corner motifs.

Much of this rug hooker's wool collection is made up of softly muted colors, and she obviously has a clear sense of her own personal palette. Opting for contrast, Mary chose a dark brown background to set off the very light gold wool that hits against its edge. The subtle shifts in tone and hue in the divisions of the corner motifs' sections call the eye to close examination. Adding some fancifulness to the overall design is the beading used to outline the scalloped edges. The palette, though it seems somewhat limited, uses colors from every color family. You will find Mary's favorite shades of green, gold, blue, and red represented in different tones and subtly varied hues.

Half Cabin, *40" x 27", #6- to 8½-cut wool on linen. Designed and hooked by Bea Brock, Kerrville, Texas, 2013.*

From first glance, Half Cabin *looks to be a hit and miss design. In actuality, it is a combination technique rug. There are mixes of browns in the outline as well as in the rusts that separate the barred sections within the squares. The central orange squares are combinations of wools, but the bars are predominantly filled with single wool pieces. On occasion, the bar colors are supplemented with close matches. The main objective employed here is to shift the values between the bars so that each one will have a visual part in the diagonal and upward movement.*

Summer Winds, *44" x 35", #6- to 8-cut wool on linen. Designed and hooked by Bea Brock, Kerrville, Texas, 2010.*

The pattern is filled with movement in the design and the areas within each motif are an open invitation to blending. The majority of woolens used here are the medium values; the darks and lights bring depth to what would otherwise be a very flat design. Look closely within each of the color fields represented here and you will see the visual texture that exists in the wide span of values. They vary in expansiveness of values, but each color space is undoubtedly enhanced by the addition of not only darks and lights, but also by variances in tone.

The mock shading used in some of the motifs invites the viewer to closely inspect the technique, especially in the center medallion. That medallion anchors the eye before it begins to move around to the other spinning motifs. The shading here is very casual and subordinates itself to the movement in the design.

All the elements float against a very dark indigo blue background that reads as a solid until the viewer is brought close to examine it. Then you see the multiple shades that range from dark teal tones to silvery blue-black and dark blue-spruce greens.

A common-colored outline is used throughout, although there are some variances in the bronze-olive wool. When using a great range of colors in a rug, this common-colored outline technique lends cohesion and keeps the composition intact.

Scrappy Patterns

CARNIVAL ROULETTE

This pattern is simply playing with circles. The daisy motif, although quite common, is filled with opportunities to really spread out an array of color. The one main criterion to keep in mind here is that the solid areas behind the daisy must offer substantial contrast. You need some sizeable pieces for the daisy, center background, outer circle background, and finally the background. Take note of the common outline being a light brown or khaki olive. With all the variety of colors found in this color sketch here, one common outline color will bring some cohesive-ness in the overall design. The hit and miss areas in the roulette will really eat into those strips that have been around for a while. The outer edge and corner motifs can be completed with a blended mix of parts and pieces in your stash. Don't forget to outline them too.

Another color plan option to consider:
Center daisy: red
Center circle: gold
Outer circle: green

PATTERN INSTRUCTIONS

These scrappy patterns will give you some simple ideas on what is possible using the most basic of tools (ruler, compass, and circle templates). In keeping with my own personal preference for wide cut, you should enlarge them to be at least 24"–30" on the shorter sides to allow for strip cuts ranging from #6 to 8. If you particularly love an extra-wide cut, you may want to consider 36" as your shorter side.

To get a clear master copy, first print the design on your home printer. Press against the book binding to flatten out the spread of pages so that your original copy is clear and complete without photo distortion.

QUILTAHOLIC

Here's another opportunity to get at those parts and pieces, but don't be afraid to splice in some of those already cut strips into the color areas if they will blend. This way you can use more of what has been lying around. Each square sports its own separate outlining; those colors are also used elsewhere as a fill color. That way the color gets spread around all across the format. Watch for good contrast between the outline and the fill color, as the outline plays an important part in the overall read of the design. Even if your colors are more muted than what I use, your results can be just as delightful. Remember to use your lights and darks to maximize every color's showmanship.

URBAN PLAZA

Though the inspiration for this pattern is Log Cabin Squares, it is transformed into a decidedly contemporary piece by virtue of its modern colors. It works well in any color palette by simply switching out the colors represented here with more antiqued or primitive colors. The purples can be changed to eggplant shades or muted plum. The orange can be changed into rusts and pumpkins. The gold can be substituted for deeper versions, hedging on browns and bronzes. Get the idea?

Search your stash for anything you might have in quantities for the backgrounds surrounding the squares and don't hesitate to blend at every opportunity to extend the colors you have. The common outline of charcoal gray used here pulls it all together; brown, muted olive, or taupe will work just fine too.

SCALLOPINE

The scallops and background will allow for plenty of blending in this design. So go through your stash and find colors that blend with each other. Be sure to pull from strips, pieces, and yardage to really get your inventory circulating. As you begin to combine colors, your rug will take on a rustic texture that is reminiscent of days gone by. Be sure to keep your outlines contrasting with the fill colors; that will add a sparkling detail to the end result. And don't think that all your outlines have to come from just one fabric. A combination of similarly valued colors for outlines will just make your rug all the more rustic.

WEBS AND WHEELS

I designed this pattern with my faithful trio of tools: ruler, compass, and circle templates. Because the motifs are broken up into wedges, and then they too are broken up with scallops, it gives you any number of options in your approach to color.

The accompanying color plan is decidedly neutral. I was inspired by all the brown wool I saw in so many stashes in the course of the last year that I decided to use them as a featured color, as opposed to just background–one more way to hone down one color that most of us have in excess.

Consider using another color in the outer scallops besides the olive I show here. Medium to dark turquoise, raspberry pink, or medium gold would work well. Or how about replacing the charcoal outline with gold? Take your pick of color plans: Try something moderately mono-chromatic, or go with an every-color-in-the-rainbow approach. Just watch for contrast all the way through, including the background, to bring it all to a glowing finish!